"Dr. Dunlop has a gift for understanding every sea: to glorify God. He shares this gift beautifully in R experience as a geriatrician with his knowledge of richer walk with the Lord during retirement. Cle; in both wisdom and compassion, this book offers encouragement and practical advice to guide us toward a retirement rooted not in the diversions of the world but in the true rest of Christ. Return to this book again and again to dwell upon Dr. Dunlop's words, grow from his insights, and praise the Lord that while our careers may end, our work for him never does."

Kathryn Butler, MD, author, *Between Life and Death*; *Glimmers of Grace*; and The Dream Keeper Saga

"In *Retiring Well*, Dr. Dunlop has given us a clear, well-organized guide to retirement. He is unafraid of sensitive topics and applies Scripture thoughtfully, including familiar passages that come to life in the context of retiring. Dunlop provides common-sense ideas that I had not thought of. Once you read it, you may well find yourself writing a new to-do list—I did.

David Wilson, Staff Member, Cru Ireland

"While many people look forward to retirement, entering this season might feel as unsettling as traveling to a foreign country where you don't know the language, customs, or terrain. Whether you're looking forward to retirement or already there, *Retiring Well* is a retirement roadmap packed with practical strategies for determining when to retire, identifying our purpose, finding balance between rest and activity, and much more. Dr. Dunlop's generous use of Scripture lays a foundation for the *why* of his counsel. This book will help readers sharpen their priorities for every area of life."

Sharon Betters, coauthor, *Aging with Grace: Flourishing in an Anti-Aging Culture*

"*Retiring Well* is a practical, well-structured guide to living your life in retirement and an excellent resource to help all of us plan for and respect the closing chapters in our life's story. It maps out logical, strategic steps so we can grow stronger in the one wellness that matters the most: our spiritual wellness. I can attest to the relevance of his wisdom to anyone anywhere in the world wishing to prepare for a rich and fruitful retirement in service to the Lord. The book is colored by Dr. Dunlop's life experiences and stories and enriched with an abundance of biblical references, so read this book with your Bible nearby.

John Povey, Director, Here to Eternity, Johannesburg, Republic of South Africa

"As one who has just begun this phase of life's journey, I am profoundly grateful for this book. The marriage of a comprehensive knowledge of Scripture, a lifetime of sober theological reflection, and decades of compassionate practice in general and geriatric medicine have made John a wise guide for those who need a mature voice to help us as we enter this chapter of our lives. John's counsel is, on the one hand, eminently practical (practicing balance while brushing your teeth) and, on the other, desperately important (more freedom to pray and time to nurture fellowship with Jesus Christ). The ten strategies outlined in *Retiring Well* will serve the serious Christian as he or she seeks faithfulness through the years of retirement. As with John's first three books, I not only enthusiastically recommend *Retiring Well*, but I will be using it!"

Mike Malone, Minister to Senior Adults, Independent Presbyterian Church, Memphis, Tennessee

"Similar to the Dunlops, we have recently made a huge change and 'retired' from what we did for more than forty years. John has synthesized wisdom drawn from his years of following Jesus, his gerontological practice, others' research, and the word of God. John addressed many of the questions we considered as well as revealed others we still must. His gentle manner comes across in print as he challenges readers to look at retirement in a countercultural way, for the sake of God's glory, which he affirms will prove to be for our good. This would be valuable reading for people approaching retirement as well as for those who love them!

Jackson and Donna Crum, Former Lead Pastor, Park Community Church, Chicago, Illinois; and his wife, Donna

"So many people stumble their way through retirement. They run out of time to put to use most of what they learn through trial and error. What a gift to have much of that experience gathered here in this wonderfully practical book by John Dunlop. Anyone retired or expecting to retire someday will be greatly blessed by reading it."

John F. Kilner, Professor Emeritus, Bioethics and Contemporary Culture, Trinity International University; author, *Dignity and Destiny*

Retiring Well

Other Crossway Books by John Dunlop

Finding Grace in the Face of Dementia

Finishing Well to the Glory of God: Strategies from a Christian Physician

Wellness for the Glory of God: Living Well after 40 with Joy and Contentment in All of Life

Retiring Well

*Strategies for Finding Balance, Setting
Priorities, and Glorifying God*

John Dunlop, MD

WHEATON, ILLINOIS

Trade paperback ISBN: 978-1-4335-7891-5
ePub ISBN: 978-1-4335-7894-6
PDF ISBN: 978-1-4335-7892-2
Mobipocket ISBN: 978-1-4335-7893-9

Library of Congress Cataloging-in-Publication Data

Names: Dunlop, John, 1947– author.
Title: Retiring well : strategies for finding balance, setting priorities, and glorifying God / John Dunlop, MD.
Description: Wheaton, Illinois : Crossway, 2022. | Includes bibliographical references and index.
Identifiers: LCCN 2021036124 (print) | LCCN 2021036125 (ebook) | ISBN 9781433578915 (trade paperback) | ISBN 9781433578922 (pdf) | ISBN 9781433578939 (mobipocket) | ISBN 9781433578946 (epub)
Subjects: LCSH: Retirees—Religious life. | Older Christians—Religious life. | Retirement—Religious aspects—Christianity.
Classification: LCC BV4596.R47 D86 2022 (print) | LCC BV4596.R47 (ebook) | DDC 248.8/5—dc23
LC record available at https://lccn.loc.gov/2021036124
LC ebook record available at https://lccn.loc.gov/2021036125

Crossway is a publishing ministry of Good News Publishers.

VP			31	30	29	28	27	26	25	24	23	22
15	14	13	12	11	10	9	8	7	6	5	4	3	2	1

To my children, Jamie, Joan, Rob, and MyunHwa,
and my grandchildren, CJ, Lucas, Carissa,
Judson, Ambrose, John, and Howard.
I pray that you live your lives with a passion for the glory of God.

Contents

Introduction

Your Opportunity to Start Fresh

THINKING ABOUT RETIREMENT? Great! I have been too. My working years have been wonderful, but very busy. Now it's exhilarating to think of being freed from the incessant activity and weight of responsibility I've carried. At the same time, the thought of retirement is somewhat intimidating. Will life after work have as much pleasure and meaning? Will I be bored?

I suspect you've been dealing with these same questions—and my prayer is that reading this book will help you toward a great retirement.

As a geriatrician, I'm a physician who specializes in the care of seniors. I frequently hear complaints from working people—especially those who follow Jesus—about the lack of balance in their lives. You may be one of those. There's much you would love to do and feel God wants you to do, but work stands in the way. You want to spend more time each day communing with God and doing good for others.

The good news is that retirement gives you the opportunity to start fresh and accomplish these things. You'll finally be able to live according to your God-given priorities and find the balance you crave.

Finding Balance in Rest and Activity

The Bible gives us two complementary emphases that are applicable to our lives in our later years: *rest* and *work*. Our challenge is to do both while keeping them in balance.

First is the privilege of rest:

Return, O my soul, to your rest;
    for the LORD has dealt bountifully with you. (Ps. 116:7)

Be still, and know that I am God. (Ps. 46:10)

Come to me, all who labor and are heavy laden, and I will give you rest. Take my yoke upon you, and learn from me, for I am gentle and lowly in heart, and you will find rest for your souls. For my yoke is easy, and my burden is light. (Matt. 11:28–30)

Rest, in this context, is not sitting around doing nothing, but taking time to pull away from the busyness of life, come to Jesus, enjoy him, and be satisfied.

Second is our need to keep active:

Not that I have already obtained this or am already perfect, but I press on to make it my own, because Christ Jesus has made me his own. Brothers, I do not consider that I have made it my own. But one thing I do: forgetting what lies behind and straining forward to what lies ahead, I press on toward the goal for the prize of the upward call of God in Christ Jesus. (Phil. 3:12–14)

Do you not know that in a race all the runners run, but only one receives the prize? So run that you may obtain it. Every athlete exercises self-control in all things. They do it to receive a perishable wreath, but we an imperishable. So I do not run aimlessly; I do not box as one beating the air. But I discipline my body and keep it under control, lest after preaching to others I myself should be disqualified. (1 Cor. 9:24–27)

Let's think about these two options—resting in Jesus and straining to serve him. Which should we emphasize?

As I ask that question, I think of the two sisters Mary and Martha, who were friends of Jesus. You likely know the story.

Now as they went on their way, Jesus entered a village. And a woman named Martha welcomed him into her house. And she had a sister called Mary, who sat at the Lord's feet and listened to his teaching. But Martha was distracted with much serving. And she went up to him and said, "Lord, do you not care that my sister has left me to serve alone? Tell her then to help me." But the Lord answered her, "Martha, Martha, you are anxious and troubled about many things, but one thing is necessary. Mary has chosen the good portion, which will not be taken away from her." (Luke 10:38–42)

I suspect that both Mary and Martha loved Jesus and wanted to please him. Martha went the road of activity; Mary chose to rest as she sat quietly with Jesus, absorbing his teaching. Jesus doesn't accuse Martha of wrong priorities. In fact, he probably enjoyed the meal she prepared. But he did commend Mary for her choice.

Mary and Martha illustrate the same tension I feel in retirement. Do I prioritize rest and enjoyment of Jesus, or is my time and energy consumed in service to God and others? The answer clearly ought to be both. The challenge is to keep them in balance.

Retiring Well is all about setting our priorities in retirement, keeping them in balance, and living according to them.

Now that I'm retired, I'm still asking the same question I asked in grade school: What should I do when I grow up? My younger friends hear that with surprise, and ask what I mean. But people of my vintage know that we have a lot of growing yet to do. We have goals to reach, and we harbor character faults that need to be dealt with. But let's face it: time may be short. This may be our last chance to grow up.

We all have heroes whom we admire and want to be like. Joe and Jan are two of mine. They're a couple in their midseventies, married for fifty years. They've both been retired for three years. Up early every morning, they individually read and study the Scriptures as they enjoy spending time with the Lord. Then they have breakfast and pray together. Each day of the week they focus on a specific subject for prayer: on Monday, their family; Tuesday, local missions; Wednesday, neighbors; Thursday, government; Friday, their friends; Saturday, world evangelism; and Sunday, their church and its leaders.

After prayer—and weather permitting—it's off for their morning two-mile walk (often combined with their prayer time). By midmorning they get into their main activity for the day. Three days a week they're at the local homeless shelter preparing and serving lunch. The other days involve a more spontaneous service project of some kind, whether to their family, church, or community.

They usually pause during the early afternoon for their major meal of the day. Some days they eat out by themselves or with friends and take advantage of the lunch specials.

The later afternoons and evenings are typically spent reading or visiting with neighbors or friends. One night each week they reserve for a date—a movie, concert, or play—and another night is spent with their home group from church. These are their closest friends, and they're diverse in age, ethnicity, education, and socioeconomic background.

Jan and Joe are spending their time well, living life in balance, impacting their worlds, bringing glory to God, and having a wonderful time doing it. You can see why they're my heroes.

My Sources

At the time of this writing, I am seventy-three. I've been in medicine for fifty-one years, practicing geriatrics most of that time. I've learned about retirement from four principal sources.

First, I've spent years enjoying the study of the Bible. Here I've learned some of God's values and priorities. I'm determined to spend my retirement in a way that reflects these values. I'll quote a lot of Scripture throughout this book, and I trust they're not just proof-texts supporting my own thinking, but representative of "the whole counsel of God" (Acts 20:27). As you encounter the numerous Scripture passages on these pages, focus on these words from God more than on what I say. That will make your reading more valuable.

Second, I've watched many of my patients retire. I've seen some do it well; they're happy and have a sense of fulfillment about changing their worlds. Others have retired poorly; they're focused on themselves and their own happiness and comfort. They're miserable, and they make everyone around them miserable. Frankly, their retirement years are wasted. I've seen all this frequently enough that I know I must approach retirement cautiously. I include many stories in this book. Most are combinations of different people's experiences to illustrate my point; some are pure fiction.

Third, I've been reading as much as I can of both Christian and secular literature to prepare for my own retirement. I've learned considerable wisdom and practical tips that I'll share with you. Many of these books are listed in the back of this book.

Fourth, I've learned from my own failures, and I continue to learn. As you read some of what I've learned, you may get the impression that I have it all together. That's far from the truth. It's much easier to dish out good-sounding advice than it is to actually live it. I confess that some of my failures are due to ongoing sin in my life. For those, I ask God to forgive me and to "create in me a clean heart, . . . and renew a right spirit within me" (Ps. 51:10). Some of my failures are due to sins I don't even recognize, and I need to pray,

> Search me, O God, and know my heart!
>   Try me and know my thoughts!
> And see if there be any grievous way in me,
>   and lead me in the way everlasting! (Ps. 139:23–24)

You'll find that this is a very personal book. I will be sharing from much of my own experience. God has richly blessed me. I was raised in a stable Christian home, and I enjoyed great privilege in my upbringing and education. God gave me a wonderful wife, and we've enjoyed almost fifty years of happy marriage. My two sons follow Jesus, have godly wives, and are raising their children well. My medical practice has blessed me with opportunities to serve as well as financial security. You may have been blessed differently throughout your life. Nevertheless, I trust that I'm not being arrogant in hoping that many of the strategies I present here are applicable regardless of your socio-economic, educational, marital, or financial background and situation. I trust that reading these strategies will be worthwhile, whatever your life is like.

If I were to share only my own wisdom, it wouldn't be worth my time to write or your time to read. Having been given better sources than my own wisdom, I pray that God will bless you in applying these thoughts to your own life, with the guidance of the Holy Spirit.

I want this book to be practical. Therefore, I'm organizing each chapter around a specific strategy to implement. I hope you can turn them into action plans for your own retirement. Before I get into those specific strategies, let's look at three prerequisites for a good retirement.

The first is financial planning. Whether you're retiring with a comfortable nest egg that will provide your needs far beyond your life expectancy, or you're living month to month, paying off loans, and eagerly awaiting each month's Social Security check, you still must do careful planning. This is an area where others have far more expertise than I do. One of the best resources is Chris Cagle's *Reimagine Retirement: Planning and Living for the Glory of God.* (See the Recommend Reading section on page 169 for more excellent books about finances). Hopefully, you've already begun your financial planning, because the sooner you begin the better.

The second thing you must do is talk to other spiritually mature friends who have retired (especially those who have retired recently). Ask their advice about how to get started. What have they learned the hard way? What advice would they give you?

The third activity you must engage in long before you retire is prayer. As with all other ventures in life, when it comes to retirement, you must make a disciplined effort to seek God's wisdom and guidance. If you're married, you should be praying about this with your spouse. Pray that you'll learn what God values and what his priorities are for you. Then begin to live by those values and priorities long before you retire.

Biblical Foundations

Scripture says very little about retirement. In fact, retirement for the average worker was unknown in biblical times. People stayed at their job as long as possible, till they died. Priests were an exception, who, according to Numbers 8:25, were to stop doing the hard physical work of preparing sacrifices at age fifty. They were then assigned to less physically demanding guard duty.

But Scripture gives us many principles for coming to the end of life well. Successfully navigating this season of life requires careful attention to these. Allow me to summarize some of this teaching to prime your thinking. I'll develop these themes further in later chapters.

God is with us to help us through our later years.

> Even to your old age I am he,
>   and to gray hairs I will carry you.
> I have made, and I will bear;
>   I will carry and will save. (Isa. 46:4)

Old age is the time to flourish and be productive.

> The righteous flourish like the palm tree
>   and grow like a cedar in Lebanon.
> They are planted in the house of the LORD;
>   they flourish in the courts of our God.
> They still bear fruit in old age;
>   they are ever full of sap and green. (Ps. 92:12–14)

We should pursue and enjoy God at all stages of life.

> How lovely is your dwelling place,
>   O LORD of hosts!
> My soul longs, yes, faints
>   for the courts of the LORD;
> my heart and flesh sing for joy
>   to the living God. (Ps. 84:1–2)

God has work for us to do for him during our senior years.

> I do not account my life of any value nor as precious to myself, if only I may finish my course and the ministry that I received from the Lord Jesus, to testify to the gospel of the grace of God. (Acts 20:24)

> Older men are to be sober-minded, dignified, self-controlled, sound in faith, in love, and in steadfastness. Older women likewise are to be reverent in behavior, not slanderers or slaves to much wine. They are to teach what is good, and so train the young women to love their husbands and children, to be self-controlled, pure, working at home, kind, and submissive to their own husbands, that the word of God may not be reviled. (Titus 2:2–5)

Jesus himself stands at the finish line of life's race to welcome us home and reward us for a life well lived. This should motivate us to finish well.

> I am already being poured out as a drink offering, and the time of my departure has come. I have fought the good fight, I have

finished the race, I have kept the faith. Henceforth there is laid up for me the crown of righteousness, which the Lord, the righteous judge, will award to me on that day, and not only to me but also to all who have loved his appearing. (2 Tim. 4:6–8)

Since we are surrounded by so great a cloud of witnesses, let us also lay aside every weight, and sin which clings so closely, and let us run with endurance the race that is set before us, looking to Jesus, the founder and perfecter of our faith, who for the joy that was set before him endured the cross, despising the shame, and is seated at the right hand of the throne of God. (Heb.12:1–2)

His master said to him, "Well done, good and faithful servant. You have been faithful over a little; I will set you over much. Enter into the joy of your master." (Matt. 25:21)

To summarize, the Bible presents us with a picture of seniors keeping active, flourishing, contributing, and setting an example for younger persons till the day God calls us to our eternal reward. These truths should encourage us to love Jesus more, and to use our retirement for his glory.

The Plan of This Book

This book is organized around ten different strategies toward a retirement that brings glory to God. These strategies will set your agenda.

1. Determine your priorities.
2. Retire at the right time.
3. Retire in the right place.

4. Take care of yourself.

5. Love God.

6. Make good friends.

7. Enjoy and strengthen your family.

8. Avoid destructive pitfalls.

9. Get busy.

10. Be flexible, adaptable, and resilient.

Don't rush though your reading, but pause frequently, think carefully, and pray that the Holy Spirit will guide you. Planning to retire to the glory of God is not easy. The questions at the end of each strategy will help you evaluate where you are and what changes you need to make.

I trust this will allow you to see that retiring in a way that brings glory to God isn't something you'll be able to do on your own. You'll need God's wisdom and help. Pause for more extended prayer as you finish reading each strategy. I give you sample prayers, but take time to pray your own. Ask God to show you how to fulfill each strategy, and then write down your specific thoughts.

Questions to Ponder

1. What gets you excited about retirement?

2. What makes you hesitant about retiring?

3. Who among your recently retired friends should you be asking about their experience and suggestions?

4. What specific prayer requests should you share with others?

5. What are you determined to do or to become in your retirement?

PRAYER

Heavenly Father, you are good, you are wise, and you have blessed me in ways far beyond anything I deserve. Now you're freeing me from the daily need to work at my job. I'm grateful for my years of employment. While working, I've been living within my comfort zone, but I haven't been able to do many of the things you or I would want. Now I'm entering a whole new world that's uncomfortable, and I'm grateful I can face it together with you. Allow me to live my life in balance, loving you and loving others. Guide my dreams, plans, and decisions about how I spend my time. Teach me your priorities so that I may live in retirement the way that glorifies you most. In addition to giving you glory I know that will give me great joy and satisfaction. I pray this in Jesus's name. Amen.

Determine Your Priorities

SID LOVED SPORTS. His year had three seasons: baseball, football, and basketball. A widower, he was seventy-eight and retired, and he had some game to watch three or four times a week. When possible, he attended games at the local college. He loved to cheer his team, especially when they got near the playoffs. All these games were his highest priority. Sid valued sports more than anything else.

I wouldn't want to discredit the value of sports, but I do wonder how Sid will look back on his later days from the perspective of eternity.

Sid teaches us the important lesson that the success of our retirement depends on what we love and make our priority. Seventeenth-century Puritan Henry Scougal wrote, "The worth and excellency of a soul is to be measured by the object of its love."[1] We must ask what Sid's love for sports says about the excellency of his soul. When planning for retirement, we demonstrate not only our personal worth but also the worth we attribute to God.

1   "Henry Scougal (1650–1678)," *A Puritan's Mind* website, accessed July 21, 2021, https://www.apuritansmind.com/puritan-favorites/henry-scougal-1650-1678/.

Setting the direction for retirement requires a clear understanding of our values, priorities, and goals. Remember the wise counsel of the great New York Yankees philosopher Yogi Berra: "If you don't know where you're going, you might not get there."[2] The Scriptures speak a lot about our priorities. But we must be aware that scriptural values and priorities are not the default of our culture. Adopting them may require us to readjust our plans. But that's okay, because living with God's priorities is our only way to joy and fulfillment.

Our Ultimate Priority

I love the concept conveyed in the Hebrew word *shalom*. It's often translated into English as "peace," but that misses some of the richness of the Hebrew. At root it means single focus, as well as oneness, totality, wholeness. Our lives are to have a single focus. Then we won't spend our time scurrying in multiple directions, which leads to anything but peace. Rather, we have peace and shalom when we clearly understand our single goal and ultimate priority, and every part of our life centers on it. We can say with Paul, "One thing I do . . ." (Phil. 3:13).

And what is that one thing? It is God's glory. Paul says, "Whether you eat or drink, or whatever you do, do all to the glory of God" (1 Cor. 10:31). It was for his glory that we were created. Through the prophet Isaiah, God describes his people as "everyone who is called by my name, / whom I created for my glory, / whom I formed and made" (Isa. 43:7). God's glory must therefore be our greatest value, our highest priority, and the overriding goal of our lives. Everything else we value must be secondary, and a means to display God's glory.

2   Yogi Berra, *When You Come to a Fork in the Road, Take It! Advice for Life from the Zennest Master of Them All* (New York: Hyperion, 2001), 53.

What is God's glory? It is his greatness, or more literally his weightiness. It isn't something we can give to God, as if we were the blazing sun giving off light and heat; we're more like the moon reflecting the sunlight. The glory of God shines into our lives, and we reflect it back to him, allowing others to see his greatness. We glorify God when we're fully satisfied with him and demonstrate that satisfaction to the people around us.

Living for God's glory makes further sense when we realize that life from start to finish isn't ultimately about us but about God. "For from him and through him and to him are all things. To him be glory forever. Amen" (Rom. 11:36). He is the origin, the means, and the goal of all things. Though our culture may tell us to find meaning in ourselves, our comfort, and our pleasure, none of these will ultimately satisfy. We can be satisfied only in the infinite resources of God. Living for God and his glory will allow us to fulfill his eternal purpose for us, to find our niche in life and be satisfied with it. This leads us to the abundant life Jesus promised: "I came that they may have life and have it abundantly" (John 10:10). Paul said much the same in teaching us to "take hold of that which is truly life" (1 Tim. 6:19). This singular focus becomes the basis for a successful, productive, and enjoyable retirement.

How do we begin to live with that as our ultimate priority? First, we must understand that our earthly bodies and lives are not our own—they belong to God: "Do you not know that your body is a temple of the Holy Spirit within you, whom you have from God? You are not your own, for you were bought with a price. So glorify God in your body" (1 Cor. 6:19–20).

We have our earthly lives only as a temporary loan from God, and we're to invest them doing things for him. Recall the story Jesus told about the rich man who went away on an extended trip and entrusted different amounts of money to the care of three servants. They were to invest and care for what he loaned them. The first two servants worked hard, earned a nice profit for the master, and gave it to him when he returned. The third was lazy and didn't invest the money. Jesus commended and rewarded the first two, while he condemned the third. In our case, the Lord has entrusted us not only with money but with life itself, including our years in retirement. We demonstrate how much we value God by how we continue loving and serving him though those years.

But to live to God's glory, we must go further and actually "die" to ourselves, as we allow our passion for Jesus to transcend our love for the things of this world.

> And he said to all, "If anyone would come after me, let him deny himself and take up his cross daily and follow me." (Luke 9:23)

> I have been crucified with Christ. It is no longer I who live, but Christ who lives in me. And the life I now live in the flesh I live by faith in the Son of God, who loved me and gave himself for me. (Gal. 2:20)

This self-denial, this dying to ourselves is particularly relevant in retirement now that we have more discretion over how we spend our time and energy. God has gifted us with these years, and he calls us to use them not for ourselves but for him. He wants us to do things that will count for eternity.

Moses, who started his life's work at age eighty and continued strong and productive for another forty years, wrote a psalm that focuses on aging. Psalm 90 ends with a prayer we should all pray each day:

Let the favor of the Lord our God be upon us,
    and establish the work of our hands upon us;
    yes, establish the work of our hands! (Ps. 90:17)

Moses's prayer is that God would take and establish what he does each day, to bring about results that will last through eternity.

If we're going to make the glory of God our highest priority, the implications are vast. Every decision we make will be affected in some way. The questions of when to retire, where to live in our retirement, and what to do in our retirement will all come down to one single question: How do we best bring glory to God? That's the question we'll think through for much of the rest of this book.

Secondary or Instrumental Priorities

Once our ultimate purpose is clearly understood, we'll have many other priorities that will allow us to accomplish it. I'll speak of these as instrumental priorities. *Instrumental* is defined as a means by which we can pursue an aim. I propose that three instrumental priorities are fundamentally applicable to all of us.

The first two are clearly stated by Jesus. When asked to name God's greatest commandment for us, Jesus responded,

You shall love the Lord your God with all your heart and with all your soul and with all your mind. This is the great and first commandment. And a second is like it: You shall love your neighbor as yourself. (Matt. 22:37–39)

There we have it: Love God with our whole beings, and love our neighbors as we love ourselves. These may seem like two separate instrumental priorities, but in practice they commonly come together, because our love for God is demonstrated as we love others, and our love for others demonstrates our love for God.

Loving God—our first instrumental priority—can take a variety of forms. It involves being quiet and delighting in his presence, hearing his voice through the Holy Spirit within us, allowing him to speak to us through the Bible as we ask him to teach and guide us through his word, and finding our joy and satisfaction in him. These are exactly the practices we may have skimped on during our working days. In consequence, we've been left feeling drained and exhausted physically, emotionally, and spiritually. When we first retire, our love for God is perhaps our greatest lack that needs to be addressed.

The second instrumental priority is to love the people around us. They may be family, our brothers and sisters at church, or community members in need. Loving them will require us to slow down, learn their needs, develop long-term relationships, and discover the best way to help them in a sustainable way. We need to equip them to provide for themselves and not create a dependence on us that destroys their initiative, dignity, and self-respect. Our goal is not to feel good about what we're doing, but to glorify God.

The third instrumental priority critical for all of us is to take good care of our bodies by doing everything we can to preserve our health and prolong our ability to glorify God. As a geriatrician, I'm fully aware that many health issues will arise over which we have no control. Nevertheless, we need to do what we can to preserve our health. This includes a healthy diet, exercise, getting enough rest, and appropriate preventive medical care. In terms of rest, remember that retirement need not and should not be a time to keep pushing to do as many things as possible. That will only put your life out of balance again. Retirement should be a time to slow down, to smell the flowers, to enjoy God and other people, and to rest. Remember that after creating the world, God rested, and he prescribed a Sabbath so that we would set aside one day in seven for God and for rest.

The word *recreation* holds within it a sense of re-creating. After working for many years, we may be worn out and in desperate need for being re-created. When we first retire, we're wise to take an extended time—several months to a year—to slow down, withdraw from the busyness of work, reprogram ourselves, and establish new life patterns for living according to our priorities. This is so important that I'll come back to it in strategy 5.

Being re-created in this sense isn't limited to physical activity, as we would customarily think of recreation. Rather, it means repairing, renewing, and reenergizing our whole beings to enable us to eventually get back into our lives and flourish. It includes creative activities, laughing, and having fun. Many people look forward to traveling in their retirement because it can provide essential re-creation. Travel provides a change of scenery that causes us to enjoy the beauty of God's creation, and also—particularly in international travel—the wealth of other cultures. If you do it early in retirement, traveling may allow a clear break from the stress of work. It's a way to press CTRL-ALT-DEL on your mind's computer, allowing you to start your retirement refreshed.

We all need these three high-tier instrumental priorities. In addition, each of us will have a list of our own instrumental priorities that will help us to accomplish the three big ones. We'll look at each of these in later strategies, but let me list some of mine to help jump-start your thinking.

1. Marriage
2. Family: children and grandchildren (our parents are with the Lord)
3. Church

4. Serving the community
5. Friends and neighbors
6. Learning

Balancing Priorities

Looking at my list, you may realize how much your failure to attend to one or more of these areas has contributed to your working-life stress, and to your lack of balance in life. You may think of areas of life that aren't on my list, areas where you haven't placed enough emphasis. Retirement will allow you to make changes and recapture life's balance. In fact, this may be one of the primary advantages of retirement. If you don't recover that balance, you may not fulfill your goal of a good retirement that truly glorifies God. It will require God's help, careful planning, and a bit of stubbornness to make it work. In retirement, if your life continues out of balance, you won't be able to blame the job; it will be your own fault.

The first weeks to months of retirement are critical to recapturing that balance and setting the direction and pace for the coming years. Initially you'll have a lot of catching up to do. Your to-do list will be long, and it will take some time to get through it before you can begin to relax. Then you'll need to reprogram yourself to live at a slower, more relaxed pace.

Take your time, slow down, and don't rush to get back into activities you intend to take up long-term. This is the time to carefully think through your other priorities, to decide where they'll fit in your retirement, and to begin to live by them. If you do this well, it will pay great dividends both in this life and the next.

Models for Retirement

We've been talking rather theoretically; now it's time to get practical. Here are several ways I've seen people retire. They've defined their priorities and kept God and his glory as their ultimate priority, but they've fulfilled this in different ways.

1. *A new career.* Pauline was a successful junior executive in a national corporation and an active member in her church. She retired at sixty-five and joined her husband, ten years her senior, in his retirement. They moved together to the farm he grew up on to embark on a life of leisure. She soon became restless, realizing that she could be doing more. They moved back to the city where they'd lived while they were working, and she enrolled in a three-year master of divinity program at a local seminary. She loved it, and then—at age seventy—took a job on the staff of her church, where she could impact the lives of many of the congregants.

2. *The excellent grandparents.* Harry retired at seventy-one as a contractor. He and his wife, Hannah, who'd been a stay-at-home mom, had two children, ages thirty-seven and forty. Their older son was a devoted follower of Jesus and had remained single. Their daughter wasn't a believer, and she'd married a man who likewise wasn't a believer. They had three children, ages two through seven, one of whom had special needs. The daughter and her husband both had full-time jobs, but they were still struggling financially. Harry and Hannah volunteered to provide childcare for all three children for seven hours daily, five days a week. They made it clear to the parents that they would be teaching the children about Jesus and introducing them to the stories contained in the Bible. Their daughter and her husband were amazed by their generosity, and though they weren't thrilled about the spiritual requirement, they gratefully accepted the offer.

3. *The permanent vacation.* John and Jennie retired from careers when they were both fifty-eight, and they bought into a beautiful retirement community. Between three golf courses, a large lake for boating, running trails, a beautiful health club,

and an active social program, their lives were full. They were enjoying themselves to the max. There was an excellent church thirty minutes away, where they were able to attend Sunday services most of the time and join in senior activities when they weren't otherwise busy. Meanwhile they stayed faithful each day to read their Bibles and pray together. They also led an evangelistic community Bible study each week, with twenty or so neighbors regularly joining them. Several came to believe in Jesus over the years.

4. *Servants of the church.* Ruben and Sylvia were both nurses and took the early retirement package they were offered by their hospital when they were both fifty-two. They were committed Christians and had always regretted having to work so many weekends, which meant they were unable to be as active in their church as they would have liked. They were determined that this would change. In retirement they immediately jumped into a slew of activities: teaching in children's church, being assistant directors of the senior's program, and helping with maintenance on the church building. For the first seven years, they were thrilled. Then they began to experience burnout. They kept going and refused to slow down—that is, until Ruben at age sixty-five had a major heart attack, which led to chronic heart failure. His disability meant that Sylvia became a full-time caregiver, and they had to stop their other activities.

5. *Phasing out gradually.* Maude had been called to missions in her thirties and spent her life trekking through the mountains of central Asia. She followed a circuit every four months, visiting and teaching in fifteen separate villages. God kept her healthy, and she maintained this routine till she was seventy-five, taking a year-long break only twice over four decades. When she finally came home, she was exhausted. Nevertheless, she began

teaching women in her church and was able to continue that for another ten years. As her strength began to fail, she stayed in her home, where she frequently invited other women to meet and talk about the Scriptures and pray together. Various people from her church cared for her until she passed into the Lord's presence.

Clearly there are advantages and disadvantages to each of these five approaches. None of them would be altogether right or wrong for everyone, and they're not mutually exclusive. Each is consistent with the ultimate priority of glorifying God, while at the same time reflecting the individual's instrumental priorities.

Questions to Ponder

1. Have your working years allowed you to place highest priority on God's glory?

2. List some instrumental priorities that have been neglected during your working years.

3. For the retirement years, what priorities of your own would you add to those I've mentioned?

4. Consider again the people mentioned in the five models of retirement given above. What priorities are they living by? Which aspects of their retirements would you like to incorporate into your retirement?

5. In light of the overall strategy we've discussed here for determining your priorities, what changes are you committed to make in your life?

PRAYER

Heavenly Father, thank you for your great love that sent Jesus to live and die for me. Thank you for saving me and allowing me to know the presence of your Spirit within. You've kept me alive to this point and allowed me to reach the time to consider retirement. Guide me through this process. I want to think the way you think and value what you value, so that my life honors you. In your grace, allow me to live the rest of my life in ways that reflect your priorities and bring you glory. Amen.

Retire at the Right Time

SALLY HAD BEEN A FAITHFUL and hardworking employee as a programmer for a tech company for forty years. At age sixty-two, she was bright, healthy, and motivated.

When her supervisor died unexpectedly, Sally felt that she qualified to be promoted to the position. However, she was passed over in favor of a younger colleague with "more years to serve the company." Sally recognized that this ageism was not only wrong but illegal. Though highly disappointed, she decided not to dispute it. She submitted her resignation and requested early retirement, which was granted. Now Sally was bright, healthy, and motivated, but unemployed—and bored.

She tried but was unable to get another programming job, and after several years started volunteering at the local library. She enjoyed this, and the clients appreciated her help, but she always felt the nagging concern that she was wasting her education and abilities. She wished that she'd kept her job.

As we get older, one of the most important questions we face is—if, in God's providence, we're given the choice—when to retire. A successful, God-honoring retirement starts with retiring at the right time.

The fact is, there's no single right age when everyone should retire. Retiring too soon may lead to boredom and wasted talent. Waiting too long may prevent us from achieving more meaningful and productive ways to serve the Lord after we retire.

Four Preliminary Questions

Retirement timing is a complex issue. Here are four basic questions to start your thinking.

1. *How is God best glorified?* In light of our ultimate goal of God's glory, a key question is this: Will God be glorified more by my continuing to work, even if my life is out of balance, or by retiring, restoring balance to my life, and then pursuing other goals? Even if you're maintaining good balance in life while working, you should ask whether retiring would allow you to achieve something even better.

2. *How is your health?* In our culture, many employers tend to look at our chronological age as the sole consideration for retirement. We've all seen it—you hit sixty-five, and you're out. This tendency is unfortunate. Our physical age is actually one of the least important considerations. In the United States it's true that you cannot begin to get Social Security or Medicare benefits till you're at least sixty-two (unless you're disabled). But in deciding when to retire, what's more important than chronologic age is what we geriatricians consider your biologic age, which depends largely on how healthy you are.

Some people in their eighties feel, look, and act like other people in their sixties, and they may have the further life expectancy of a sixty-year-old. Their biologic age is therefore more like sixty than eighty. It can go the other way as well—some people in their sixties have aged rapidly, and they look and act like those who are much older. It's biologic age, not chronologic age, that should be relevant in deciding the time of retirement.

Another thing to consider—especially if you aren't in the greatest health—is the possibility that retiring sooner, and living with less stress and a healthier lifestyle, could allow for a longer life and more productive years.

3. *Are you prepared financially?* Though critically important, as mentioned earlier, I defer to writers who have greater expertise on this than I have. (See the recommended reading list at the end of this book.)

4. *Are you at peace in your heart that the age at which you're thinking about retiring is God's best for you?* Whereas there are many decisions we make in life where we don't need to inquire about God's will (since in the Bible he has already stated his will for us in those areas), the time of retirement is not one of them. (We'll discuss this further in strategy 8.)

Is Your Retirement Voluntary?

Not everyone has the privilege of retiring voluntarily. In fact, one study showed that 47 percent of retirements were *not* voluntary.[1] It may be forced upon you by the company you work for, perhaps as you reached a mandatory retirement age, or when your job was eliminated by corporate downsizing, a merger, or economic downturn. For others, health issues—either their own or of someone they love and need to be with—have precipitated retirement.

When retirement isn't voluntary, those who are forced into it may not feel ready, either financially or emotionally. In those

---

1 Phyllis Diamond, "Facing Forced Retirement: Getting Upright When Your World Turns Upside Down" in *The Retirement Challenge: A Non-Financial Guide from Top Retirement Experts*, by various members of the Retirement Coaches Association (Robert Laura, 2018), loc. 702, Kindle.

situations, you may need to apply some of the principles of strategy 10 that discuss adapting and resilience.

Hopefully you're among those whose retirement is voluntary and planned well in advance, and you're ready for a change. You'll have your own reasons for choosing when to retire, but I find that for many, it again comes down to being able to achieve life balance. You're itching for the freedom to live by your own priorities and set your own agenda.

On the other hand, now may not be the wisest time for you to retire voluntarily. Some don't have the financial ability to retire when they may otherwise want to, and they're grateful for the opportunity to continue to work. They can go on fulfilling their other financial commitments, building up their retirement funds, defer living off savings, and allow their eventual Social Security payout to increase.

Others may be feeling an obligation to retire for a variety of inadequate reasons. For example, they may assume that because they're turning sixty-five, it's time to retire, even though they're still productive, enjoying work, and not emotionally ready to leave the workplace. That's the way I felt when I retired at sixty-seven from the clinic where I'd worked for thirty-eight years. Though I knew I needed to slow down, I wasn't ready emotionally to give up medicine entirely. Why change and ruin a good thing?

Some have no particular reason they must retire; they're happy and content on the job. But when they stop and think about retirement, they come up with a list of things they would like to do if only they had more free time. The issue for them isn't necessarily what they're doing on the job, but what that job is keeping them from doing. In retirement, they'll have the freedom to live according to their own priorities.

Advantages of a Younger Retirement

The age of a younger retirement is of course relative. I know of one man who was successful in the world of finance and retired to a life of affluent leisure at age thirty. I have friends retiring in their late seventies who are still healthy, strong, and capable of working several more years. I would put them in the category of "younger retirement." I would label anyone as "young" who can retire before they're forced to do so by age-related reasons.

Here are some of the advantages of a younger retirement.

Balance

Since one of the benefits of retirement is the freedom it provides to get life back into balance, then assuming you have the finances, discipline, and motivation to do it, the sooner you can retire and achieve that balance the better.

For many (including myself), work has forced them to be up and out of the house at an early hour, limiting their significant time with the Lord. Others have had to work weekends and been deprived of church fellowship. Those working at desk jobs may not have had time to exercise, and they've gotten out of shape physically. Work for others is a constant preoccupation to the point that it interferes with their sleep or their ability to enjoy other parts of life. Being so consumed by work leaves them stressed out, irritable, and emotionally drained. That's hardly a way to bring God glory. Retirement will free them from that stress, allowing them to live by their own priorities in a way that truly puts first things first.

Ministry

Retirement may open opportunities to serve God in totally new ways for you as an individual, or as a couple if you're married.

I've been privileged in recent years to share with senior groups in a number of churches across the country. I find it interesting that the leaders of these groups—who in many cases are full-time pastors of seniors—are individuals or couples who've taken early retirement to allow for this career change. Some have retired early enough to pursue further training to equip them for this ministry. But there will be many opportunities to serve that won't require formal training yet permit years of immense productivity for God and his kingdom.

I've known several couples who retired in their fifties to spend the next twenty years in international missions. Some had already lived in their new home country and knew the language and culture well. For others, such a move required several years of training and learning a new language—not something you typically embark on at sixty-five. If you wait too long, these international ministry opportunities will become fewer—so to make a change like this, you need to do so while still healthy and energetic.

In summary, retiring early may allow more productive years of service.

Recovering from Fatigue and Burnout

As we age, our strength, energy levels, and cognitive abilities will usually begin to wane. We may feel weary and burned out, having lost zip, enthusiasm, and creativity. It's even possible to be "weary of doing good" (Gal. 6:9). Work performance and productivity may decline, and that not only becomes depressing but may also become a poor witness for our Lord.

While the wisdom and experience gained over the years may partially compensate for any decline, it may be wise to quit while our performance is still close to "the top of our game." If we continue to work beyond that point, we may make errors, harm others, and bring shame on ourselves and our Lord.

Time to Enjoy

God wants us to take time to enjoy the blessings he abundantly pours on us. The apostle Paul affirms that God "richly provides us with everything to enjoy" (1 Tim. 6:17). An earlier retirement may allow you to enjoy some of those blessings.

Some people talk about their bucket lists, a phrase made popular in the 2007 comedy film *The Bucket List* starring Morgan Freeman and Jack Nicholson. Two terminally ill men decide to forgo treatment and together come up with a list of crazy things they want to do before they die. They enjoy every minute, and come to the end of their lives with a sense of completion. That's hardly a God-honoring approach to the end of our earthly journey. However, the idea of fulfilling a list of things we want to experience and enjoy during our lives will provide reasons to praise him and contribute to his glory. We must be cautious to wisely draw up our bucket list, and avoid reckless and risky activities like those depicted in the movie.

Marriage and Family

Our working years can often be stressful on marriages and on our relationships with adult children and grandchildren. Retirement will ideally provide the opportunity to spend more enjoyable, satisfying, and spiritually productive time together.

If one of your goals is to be able to significantly impact the younger generation for God's kingdom, then the more time you have after retirement, the better. Meanwhile, when it comes to grandchildren, remember that the younger they are, the more impressionable they are.

Don't Retire Too Early

Early retirement may sound attractive—but be careful. There are several things to consider before you choose to retire voluntarily, since work may be more valuable to you than you realize.

God Designed Us for Work

Remember, God himself "worked." He did the work of creation before he paused to rest. He also designed us as humans to work.

Adam had a job to do in caring for Eden before sin entered the world. His work was pleasurable and productive. What sin introduced was not the fact of work but the onerous character of work.

We see numerous examples in Scripture of people working well into their older years. Consider Moses, who embarked on his life's work at eighty. Caleb, at eighty-five, was anxious to take on a new challenge. Job must have been well into his years when he had to pick up from scratch to restart his life.

In their book *How to Finish the Christian Life: Following Jesus in the Second Half,* George Sweeting and his son Don speak of the "retirement rebels" who are willing to break out of the mold of their culture and continue to work.[2] This doesn't necessarily require that they continue their present jobs; it may be appropriate to continue to work but with a change of pace, or to move into a volunteer role.

Calling

Many are working with a conviction that God has called them to what they're doing.

My personal story was rather dramatic. I started college without a clear sense of direction. I sincerely wanted to spend my life

2   Donald W. Sweeting and George Sweeting, *How to Finish the Christian Life: Following Jesus in the Second Half* (Chicago: Moody, 2012), 59.

doing whatever God would "call" me to. Meanwhile, I assumed I would join my father in his business.

In registering for my junior year, I felt that I should take accounting—a course that wasn't required for my degree or one that I particularly wanted to take. During the week I had to register for the upcoming collegiate year, I asked the Lord to let me know if he had a different direction for me, and I asked that he do this before I invested any time studying accounting.

During that week, three separate individuals—none of whom knew what I was thinking and praying about—approached me to say they thought I should go into medicine. They weren't consciously speaking for God, but in the context of my prayer, I heard God's call loud and clear.

Now—fifty-three years later—I've never regretted my life in medicine. As I was thinking about retiring, I half-heartedly said that I wish I'd asked those impromptu advisers exactly how long that call to medicine was good for. But now, it's with significant trepidation that I forsake such a clear call. I only do it knowing that my abilities are diminishing, and I'm confident that God will call me to a new area consistent with my capabilities.

Stewardship

By God's providence, you've likely developed an enviable expertise in your career. You're more capable at your job than anyone around you. God has placed you in a position of leadership, and you have the respect of many. This allows you to teach and influence others. This is a gift from God that you've been entrusted with to steward well and use for his glory.

Furthermore, you're likely earning your peak salary. You may need that money to build up your nest egg, but even if you've met your financial goals already and have enough saved, you can generously give from your current salary to help meet the needs of others. Remember Paul's challenge to the rich that they "be generous and ready to share" (1 Tim. 6:18–19).

Structure

We all need some degree of structure in our lives to be productive. We need to know what we're supposed to do each day, so that, like it or not, we get up and get going. Without such structure we may become inefficient and waste time.

Continuing to work, despite its downsides, provides that structure. Sure, we pay a price for it, since we really enjoy days that aren't planned and that allow us freedom to do what we want. But such freedom can get old quickly.

Friends and Social Connections

Many working people find most of their social relationships at work. These are the people they share coffee breaks and lunches with. They know each other's families, their heartaches, and their joys. These connections will be hard to maintain without the constant interaction of working together. Once retired, it will take a lot of time and effort to build new and equally close friendships.

Another consideration for many followers of Jesus is that, except for their friends at work, they may have no friends who aren't believers. The workplace is their primary arena for living out and sharing the gospel evangelistically.

Dependence

Those who work for large corporations are typically dependent on the company to do many personal things they'll miss in retirement. They've always had someone else who would fix their computer, invest their retirement funds, provide their health insurance, and even manage their schedules. And the higher they are on the corporate ladder, the more numerous are the personal services they've enjoyed. Retirement will require them to be independent and do all these things on their own.

Meaning and Accomplishment

We all need a sense of meaning and accomplishment in our lives. For many, this is derived from their work. Unless it's replaced once we're retired, that loss of meaning may lead to depression.

I once heard someone say, "My life has no real meaning since I retired. I used to do things that had an impact on the world, and now I just do things that are supposed to make me happy and fill my time." I could sympathize with him, but the problem wasn't retirement itself, but rather how he was spending his time. He needed to get busy and find meaningful things to do to replace what he had at work. This will come in strategy 8.

Identity

Many of us find our sense of identity in our work. It's the way we view ourselves, and it's how we want others to see us.

When talking about retirement with a patient, I sometimes would innocently ask, "And what do you do?" I found the answers generally came in two ways. Those in one group would say they worked for such and such a company. Those in the other group would say they were a teacher, doctor, pastor, and so on. This latter group—those who identified themselves by their profession—can have an especially difficult time adjusting to retirement. Work has provided them a high level of responsibility and esteem. They've been able to contribute much to others, and they've hopefully done it in a way that honors God. Is that bad? Normally not.

But the danger may be that they've begun to view themselves as better than they ought.

Basing our identity on our profession, abilities, or accomplishments is often evidence of sinful pride. To God, our identity is primarily that of being made in his image and redeemed by Christ. How much greater is that than anything we do! Giving up our work identity may be difficult, and learning to find our identity only in Christ may be quite humbling—but that's precisely what we need. When we no longer have a profession to identify with, people might not assume how capable or smart we are. We must begin to follow more closely Jesus's instructions in the Beatitudes (Matt. 5:3–11) about becoming "poor in spirit," mourning our pride, among other things, and having a hunger and thirst for righteousness. The loss of work identity associated with retirement may be difficult, but God can use it to allow good results in our spiritual transformation.

Disappointment

More than half of active workers want to work longer than full retirement age. Further, 39 percent of those over sixty-five who retired later went back to work—either out of boredom or a desire to be more useful.[3]

A carefree retirement isn't always as wonderful as we expect. That's not necessarily all bad, since a new post-retirement job may be less intense, allowing people to achieve more balance in their lives, and it might be more fulfilling, focusing more on service and less on making money.

For some, dissatisfaction in retirement may have spiritual roots. They may have failed to slow down and find fulfillment in God.

---

3 Horner, "The Right Work Can Keep You Young," in *The Retirement Challenge*, loc. 323, Kindle.

Still, it raises the question: Would it have been better for them to stay at their job?

Addiction

Work itself can be addicting. It gets our adrenaline and endorphins pumping. Without work, we can feel as if we're wasting our time and become depressed. If you're a driven, type-A person, it would be wise to find another way to satisfy those needs, or retirement will drive you and those around you crazy.

———

So, when should you retire?

Both early and later retirements have their pros and cons. Your current employment may be doing more for you than providing a paycheck, but the freedom to pursue your own priorities may be enticing. To have a good retirement, it's essential that you carefully think through these issues before you plan your retirement date.

Some will have the opportunity to retire gradually. My wife and I have both been blessed to do that. Dorothy and I were living in the Chicago area. I was sixty-seven and ready to back off from the full-time practice of medicine. Dorothy was sixty-four, working as a medical researcher and as a full professor at a medical school.

Upon my first retirement, we moved to Connecticut to be near family. I wasn't ready to quit medicine, and had already arranged to work three days a week seeing patients and doing some teaching in a medical school. Dorothy was allowed to work remotely from our new home, and now is working in a phased retirement where, for her last two years, she works two-and-a-half days a week. Being allowed to gradually cut back in these ways has been a blessing.

It has allowed us to recapture balance and begin to explore ways to engage in the next chapter of our lives.

If gradual retirement is an option for you, I strongly recommend it. But even if you retire gradually, it's wise at some point to make a clean break from work, to review your priorities, and to carefully decide your next steps.

Questions to Ponder

1. What does your work give you that you consider to be of the highest value?

2. What activities is your work keeping you from doing?

3. How much does your sense of identity come from your work?

4. Will you be able to do things after retirement that will glorify God in greater ways than you're now doing while working?

5. In light of what we've discussed for this strategy of retiring at the right time, what changes are you committed to make in your life?

PRAYER

Father, you have been gracious in allowing me to work all these years. As I contemplate retirement, I need your wisdom. The idea of retiring and being free to pursue my own priorities is attractive, but unless my priorities become your priorities, I know I'll be wasting my time.

I pray that you'll lead me to retire at the right time in ways to glorify Jesus in the greatest way possible. Amen.

Retire in the Right Place

IN DETERMINING OUR ABILITY to successfully glorify God in retirement, the choice of where to live is likely second only to the decision about when to retire. There's a lot to think about.

First, finances. Some will be blessed with the resources to live anywhere they want. Others will have financial constraints that limit their options.

Whatever your level of financial resources, the two big decisions involve (1) what type of living situation (whether private home, condo, retirement community, etc.), and (2) in what geographic location.

Before we get into details, I'll mention three general considerations.

Social Connections

The quality of our retirement and ability to glorify God in these years will largely depend on the social relationships we develop and maintain. These will include family and friends, both Christian and non-Christian. Our living situation will have a lot to do with our ability to make and maintain these friendships.

Some of us will place a high priority on having close friendships with non-Christians, whereas others will feel God's call to minister to and encourage those who already follow Jesus.

Good friends contribute not only to the quality of our retirement years but also to our longevity. Without close relationships people simply die younger.[1]

We should make it a goal to live where it's easy to make friends and spend meaningful time with them.

Church

Wherever we choose to live, an important consideration is our ability to get to a strong church.

There may never be a better church for you than the one in which you're currently established, and you may be wise to live where you can continue in that fellowship. This is true especially if your closest friends are there, you're flourishing under the teaching, and you can continue in a ministry that God is blessing.

If you begin attending a new church in a new community, it may take years to rebuild the friendships and ministries you now have. Keep in mind, however, that churches (like everything else) will change over time, and what may be best today may not always be best.

Adaptability

The choice of our living situation may determine our ability to adapt to changes in our functional capacities that will inevitably come with age. Walking, climbing stairs, driving, shopping,

1   Joel Shuflin, "Mates: Don't Retire without Them," in *The Retirement Challenge: A Non-financial Guide from Top Retirement Experts*, by various members of the Retirement Coaches Association (Robert Laura, 2018), loc. 1276, Kindle.

cooking, and maintaining the home will all potentially become limited as time goes on.

It's unlikely that any decision about the type of living situation you first choose when you retire will continue to be best as time goes on. You'll likely need to make at least one future move during your retirement.

Living Options

Let's think about some of the pros and cons of available options. As you consider these possibilities, keep in mind that whereas you can serve God anywhere you live, some situations may be more conducive than others.

Staying in Your Long-Term Home

Staying where you are may be the easiest and most comfortable option. You know your neighbors and the local community. You are established in your church and regularly taking part. Hopefully, you already have a Christian ministry, and you're reluctant to give that up. You also have your favorite food store, bakery, hairdresser, doctor, dentist, lawyer, financial planner, and bank. Your family may live nearby. If you move, it will be difficult—and take years—to replace these essential people and services in an equivalent way.

Another advantage of staying in the long-term home is that you often have more space than you need, which opens the possibility of allowing people with financial needs to live with you. It may be your children and/or their families. Combining your finances with others living with you may be a boon to everyone. Their presence can also provide you with needed help around the house and maximize your opportunities for meaningful interaction with children and grandchildren.

After our sons left home, we asked students from the local seminary to live in our home. It allowed us to get to know and be enriched by these wonderful people. They had free housing, we appreciated their help in many ways, and it was comforting to have someone in the house when we were away. It was a win-win.

On the other hand, there are downsides to staying in your home. Life has been focused for decades on accumulating things, and it may be that your home is cluttered with items you don't need and will never use. If nothing is done to clean up this clutter, it will continue to collect dust until you choose to do something about it—or until God takes you home. Moving out of your long-term home is an inducement to eliminate stuff. If you don't deal with it, eventually someone else—often your children—will have the difficult task of making decisions about your possessions. Moving out of your home and getting rid of things now can be a wonderful gift to your children. Also consider that maintaining your own home will likely become more difficult and more expensive as the years go by. That responsibility, too, will likely eventually fall on someone else.

Something else to think about is that if you happen to lose the ability to drive, living in a private home can be very isolating, and it can force you to depend more on others. Not being able to get out may cripple any Christian ministry you have. Furthermore, life changes. Friends move away, stores close, doctors, lawyers, and hairdressers retire. None of them can be relied on forever.

But not everyone is ready to leave one's home. When I suggested to a dear friend that it was time to leave his beautiful home, he took my hand and said, "John, though this house is my greatest source of problems, it's also my greatest source of energy." I made a similar suggestion to another dear friend. She tearfully responded, "I cannot do that. My deceased husband and

I worked together to build our house when he returned from the Second World War. We raised our children and lived our lives here. It's the only thing that ties me to him. I will not leave those memories." I could only quietly respond by saying, with tears in my eyes, "I hear you."

Today's world provides a number of services to allow seniors to live at home. In-home maintenance services, meals-on-wheels, home-based medical care, and easily accessible transportation can make it easier to live in your home for years to come.

Putting off the decision to leave your long-term home is reasonable, but keep in mind that a move like this is a lot of work. The younger and more physically and mentally capable you are, the easier it is. If you put if off too long, most of the work and mental strain will have to be assumed by others. Further, the longer you put it off, the less time you'll have to enjoy your new situation and make it into a place where you can feel at home.

Moving In with Children—or Children Moving In with You

Moving in with one of your children's families or their moving in with you are other options that have many advantages. They save money, and have the same benefits we experienced with seminary students.

But there are some disadvantages. If there are grandchildren in the home, there's probably a lot of commotion. Or the family may be gone a lot, which may mean you'll be left alone. It may also be difficult if you don't feel truly at home in their place (or they don't make you feel at home).

Downsizing to a Smaller Residence Nearby

One of the excellent alternatives to continuing to live in your long-term home is to downsize to a smaller and perhaps newer home, one that needs less maintenance but is still in the same community. An apartment or condo instead of a freestanding house can provide most of the maintenance and many other services. As you anticipate a time when you can no longer handle stairs, finding a single-level home is helpful. A move like this also forces you to reduce your clutter.

The practical benefits of downsizing should be clear, but there may also be a spiritual value, as the move begins to free you from your attachment to things of this world. We'll return to these spiritual values in strategy 5. Of further spiritual value is the fact that condos and apartments often put you in closer contact with neighbors. This allows for more diverse friendships and provides relationships in which you can be living out and sharing the gospel.

Downsizing typically saves you money in taxes and mortgage. Depending on the location, condo or apartment living may allow you easier access to essential services—a wonderful benefit when your mobility decreases (for example, when you're no longer driving).

In our transition between Illinois and Connecticut, Dorothy and I had a condo in downtown Chicago close to Dorothy's office. Our building had an elevator and a grocery store, pharmacy, post office, hardware store, bank, lap pool, exercise room, and restaurant. Because it was across the street from a university hospital, there were doctor's offices for most specialties, physical therapy, X-ray, and lab work. It was literally a city within the city. Residents could live there without ever having to go outside. And many did.

The other advantage of downsizing is that it may allow you to be debt free. Selling your home and using the equity to purchase something less expensive—or investing the equity and renting with the interest—may give you more financial freedom.

Retirement Communities

Another option is moving to a retirement community. This frequently involves relocating to a totally new geographic area, building a new group of friends, and finding a new church and new ways to serve the Lord.

Many retirement communities are for active younger seniors, and they provide private homes that are owned or rented by the resident. Like a condo, the community provides all exterior upkeep and landscaping, along with many activities such as golf, tennis, a swimming pool, hiking trails, and an extensive social program. They have large community centers that often include a restaurant. There are ample opportunities to serve Christ by participating in community events or Bible studies, as well as enjoying relaxed time with fellow residents, both believers and nonbelievers.

Other retirement communities are designed for less independent seniors, and provide private suites or small apartments in larger buildings. Under the same roof will be a nice dining room that offers at least one meal each day, as well as exercise facilities. Monthly fees will include meals, housecleaning, and basic 24/7 medical presence. Most will allow residents to pay for higher levels of assistance with daily living activities such as dressing, bathing, preparing meals, and taking medications. In addition, many of these communities provide rehab and nursing home care on site.

My parents lived in this type of community. I was particularly impressed with the value of having a nursing home in the same building when Dad fell and broke his hip. After being cared for in a hospital, he was moved to the rehab unit for six weeks. I was with him one day for about four hours. During that time he had six visitors, all residents from the community. I commented to Mom that I cared for many residents in freestanding nursing homes who were lucky to have six visitors in a year. My parents enjoyed the years they had in this retirement community, and we enjoyed visiting them. The atmosphere was warm and inviting, the food was excellent, and it was fun to meet their fascinating friends.

Retirement communities can provide significant opportunities to serve the Lord in an entirely new mission field. One of my friends, a retired missionary who moved to a retirement community in Florida, assured me that if you made this type of move with a mindset for ministry, you could be sure to find it. Without that vision, it could be a spiritual wasteland. He and his wife have become known for their kindness and caring. Now in his eighties, he leads an evangelistic Bible study and is frequently called on by people in spiritual need. He regularly does hospital visits and funerals. Last year he even officiated at a wedding.

Some retirement communities are specifically Christian. They provide wonderful opportunities for spiritual nurture and fellowship, but they may not offer as many opportunities for evangelism.

For all the advantages of retirement communities, there are also disadvantages. First is that they're quite expensive and not covered by most insurance policies. Second is that they typically offer little age diversity (the same is true regarding diversity in socioeconomics, education, and ethnicity). I sometimes hear people say, "I don't want to live with a group of old people like me." I've personally learned that I thrive and grow most when I'm with people younger than me. I absorb their enthusiasm, and sometimes I share with them things God has taught me.

Assisted Living

Assisted-living facilities are becoming very popular. They offer a variety of services, so it's difficult to say exactly what they're like. Typically, you pay a monthly charge for a studio apartment with a small kitchenette and bath. At least one meal is offered each day (many will offer three). Large common areas encourage residents to spend time socializing out of their apartments. Often regularly scheduled activities occur off the grounds of the facility, as well as exercise programs. All have an on-site nursing presence 24/7, and when needed, residents can contract for more supervision of their medications, and hire personal aides.

Many assisted-living facilities have specific areas for patients suffering from dementia. These patients are confined to a safe environment, and the staff is especially trained in dementia care.

Assisted-living facilities share all the downsides of retirement communities. In addition, since they don't include a nursing home or rehab facility, residents must go to other facilities when further care is needed.

Since none of these options may be sufficient for all stages of retirement, it may be well to think in terms of several stages. In addition to deciding what living arrangement is best early in retirement, it may be wise to do some long-term contingency planning.

Dorothy and I currently live in a condo. We love spending time with neighbors, entertaining friends, and being close to family. But we're already thinking about a senior living community where we could move one day, one that offers more care for when we're less independent.

If you think that's a possibility for you, keep in mind that such facilities are expensive, so it's wise to consider that in your long-range financial planning.

Where to Live?

Once you have an idea of the kind of residence you would like to live in, it's time to think about the geographical location. Dorothy and I felt that it was important to become established in the community where we could live out our lives while we were still relatively healthy. We wanted to make friends, build a mutual support system, get established in a church and ministry, and make a contribution to our new community while we were still able. We knew family would be increasingly important as we came to the end of life, so we decided to make a move to be nearer to them early in retirement. The question was, Where?

Here are five things to consider when determining where to retire.

Climate

The older people get, the more sensitive we are to the cold, which is why so many either move south permanently, or at least winter in warmer climes if they can afford two residences.

That works well for some, but I've known many of these "snowbirds" who never fully settle in either place, and life becomes disjointed. I also know some who were thrilled with their lives in the warmer climes in their sixties and seventies, but as they got into their eighties and became more dependent, they moved back to their original communities. Unfortunately, they found that their friends were no longer there, and things had changed so much that they didn't feel they belonged and were rather lonely.

I'm frequently asked why we moved from Chicago to New England. My answer is that we put more value on being close to kids and grandkids than on weather.

Family

I recently asked a friend and his wife, both about to retire, if they were going to stay in the area or move elsewhere. He responded that his two sons lived six doors away from each other in the South. Then he smiled and said, "We don't have a choice!" My response was, "And you probably don't want one either."

We chose family as our deciding priority when we left our Chicago home and moved to the East Coast. Both of our sons and their families were in the East, one in Connecticut and the other in Washington, D.C. We felt particularly blessed to have both families in reasonable proximity to each other. Our new residence was less than a mile from one son and a five-hour drive or train ride to the other. We love both of them, as well as their wives and children. We enjoy our grandchildren and the opportunity to share in their formative years.

Cost of Living

The cost of living varies greatly from one region of the country to another. For example, it costs 30 percent less to live in rural Alabama than where I live in New Haven, Connecticut. This can be a significant factor in your decision of where you want to live.

These comparisons are accessible online.[2]

Urban, Suburban, or Rural?

The type of community you choose will significantly impact your life. Living in a rural or suburban setting typically provides a more relaxed and slower lifestyle. It may allow you a deeper

---

2 Extensive data for making cost of living comparisons among U.S. cities is available at the *Cost of Living Index* website of the Council for Community and Economic Research, https://www.coli.org/.

relationship with a small number of friends. But it requires you to be more independent, and it tends to put you with a group of people who in many ways are like yourself.

Urban living has a faster pace, offers more activities like plays and concerts, and potentially provides a more diverse group of friends.

We chose to compromise and live in a small city. We also made it a priority to live near a large university. We wanted to be able to enjoy the cultural events and intellectual activities, such as community lectures offered by the academic community. It's wonderful to be able to interact with students from a wide variety of backgrounds and disciplines. And our church enriches us through its diverse membership.

Ministry

You can live for the Lord anywhere in the country, or for that matter anywhere in the world. However, there will be a lot of regional variation as to the type of ministry in which you can be involved.

Living in the city may put you in closer contact with the social problems often found in urban areas. Poverty, homelessness, and drug addiction all provide service opportunities. Ministry in the Midwest or in the Bible Belt may look considerably different than in New England or in the Northwest.

Making the Choice

With all these considerations, how do we go about deciding where to live?

Once again, there are no cut-and-dried answers. This is an area where we need to seek God's wisdom. Start with praying for that wisdom. Have long talks in person or by phone with people who've chosen different options. See what went into their decisions, and how things turned out for them.

Talk to your spiritual leaders, trusted Christian friends, and family to get their counsel. Then make a decision, recognizing that few decisions are irreversible.

Questions to Ponder

1. How long do you feel you could safely live in your present home?

2. If you became more dependent on others, would you have the necessary support to allow you to continue in your home? Would that be a burden on others?

3. How important is it to you to move to a place where you could live for the rest of your life without having to make another move?

4. What are the most important considerations for you in deciding which region of the country to live in?

5. In light of what we've discussed for this strategy of retiring in the right place, what changes are you committed to make in your life?

PRAYER

Gracious Father, I know that where I choose to live is critical to how I will fulfill the priorities you have for me in my retirement years. But because there are so many unknowns and variables, I don't feel entirely capable of making a good decision.

I'm glad that I can depend on you for your wisdom and guidance to choose what is best. And Father, if I make an unwise choice, give me the humility and wisdom to reverse it.

Wherever I live, I pray that you'll give me opportunities to glorify you. I pray this for your glory and my good. Amen.

Take Care of Yourself

AN ESSENTIAL WAY to maximize how our retirement years can bring glory to God is to take care of the body and mind he has entrusted to us.

Paul tells us that our bodies are not our own, but are the temples of the Holy Spirit and are to be used to glorify God (1 Cor. 6:19–20). During our working years, we may have begun to "go soft" physically and to become overstressed emotionally. We may not have been able to get enough sleep. And now, going into retirement, we have a lot of changes to make.

Mentally, it may be just the opposite for you. Work may have continuously stimulated your brain, and without due effort retirement may cause you to go soft mentally.

Remember that a premature and preventable death will not contribute to your ability to glorify God in this life. In Psalm 6, David reminded God, "In death there is no remembrance of you; / in Sheol who will give you praise?" (Ps. 6:5). Start taking better care of yourself early in retirement, and you may have more years to be productive.

Physical Health

All too often, our jobs keep us from healthy practices. We don't get enough exercise on the job or have the energy or time to stay in shape when we're not working. Sometimes our jobs involve too many large meals or snacks, and we've put on too much weight. As a result, our blood sugars may start creeping up, and we start down the road to diabetes. Work stress may lead to hypertension. Sedentary living causes muscles to get flabby, and it gets harder and harder to engage in the activities required to get in shape and lose weight.

Hopefully, retirement will provide a wake-up call, and we can begin to make healthy lifestyle changes. These will allow us to recapture some of the strength and energy we'll need for a productive and lengthy retirement.

The first step should be to visit a primary care practitioner, if we haven't done this in the last year or so. A general checkup should be done that includes several important steps.

1. Review current problems you're experiencing as well as your medications. I have a professional bias here; one of my goals as a geriatrician is to get my patients off as many medications as possible, since the elderly may be more prone to side effects. I half-jokingly tell my patients that pills are poisons with a few good side effects. It's wiser to avoid medications whenever it's possible to manage problems with lifestyle changes instead.

2. "Know your numbers." Do you know what your blood pressure and blood sugar levels are? Do you know how many steps you take in the average day? How does your current weight compare to your ideal weight? What are your cholesterol levels, and the breakdown between the good HDL and bad LDL?

The common problems found in this checkup include obesity, diabetes, high blood pressure, high cholesterol, and osteoporosis. If any of these are found, ask if you need any specific lifestyle changes or medications.

3. Discuss prevention. Do you need screening for osteoporosis, colon cancer, or breast cancer? Have you had a general blood chemistry analysis in the last few years? What about immunizations? At sixty-five you should have received two different kinds of pneumonia shots, plus the newer shingles shot and its booster, plus an every-ten-year diphtheria, tetanus, pertussis (DPT) shot, as well as a vaccination against COVID-19, and a yearly high-dose flu shot.

Even if your weight, blood sugar, and cholesterol levels are good, look at your diet. Avoid fatty red meats and starches, and instead move toward a plant-based Mediterranean diet.

If you're currently taking medications, you may also ask if making lifestyle changes would allow you to safely get off them.

4. When you're with your medical professional, talk about advance directives. These are legal documents that allow you to indicate the care you would want to receive in the event of devastating illness. In most states these are available online and can be filled out without legal assistance. Search advance directives and then the two-letter abbreviation for your state—for example, "Advance Directive NY."

The names and kinds of documents may vary from state to state, but in most cases they should include a limited power of attorney. Here you appoint the person you want to make decisions for you if you become incapacitated. This should be someone who's likely going to be available, who knows you well enough to be able to anticipate what you would want, and who is able to make an emotionally difficult decision, such as discontinuing life support.

Another document that's included should be a living will, which basically outlines your choices about receiving aggressive life-sustaining treatment when there's little hope of significant recovery.

The third document, a "Do not resuscitate" order, or DNR, should be carefully thought through before signing. Personally, I wouldn't recommend a DNR while you're in reasonably good health and living a productive life. If your health is such that you don't want resuscitation, a DNR may be appropriate. Before signing a DNR, check with your doctor's office, as most states now have a newer form that requires a professional's signature; it becomes a medical order, and will more effectively prevent unwanted life support.

5. Ask whether it's safe to immediately begin an exercise program, or if you should first take tests, such as a stress test. Once you have your physician's approval, the next step is to establish a plan to regain and maintain your fitness. If you have any questions about how to do this, it may be wise to consult an athletic trainer geared to seniors.

Unfortunately, our culture is basically lazy. We would rather take pills than exercise. One of my favorite quotes is from geriatrician Robert Butler: "If exercise could be packed in a pill, it would be the single most widely prescribed and beneficial medicine in the nation."[1] But it's much better if we get out of our seats and move. We need four basic types of exercise:

Aerobic exercise includes anything that gets your heart rate up, and perhaps causes you to break a sweat. You can take a brisk walk, jog, or swim, but even housecleaning and gardening are adequate if you're really going at it. A reasonable approach is

1   Robert N. Butler, "Exercise: The Neglected Therapy," *The International Journal of Aging and Human Development*, 8, no. 2 (1977–1978).

doing something aerobic for at least three hours each week. The current recommendations of doing ten thousand steps each day may seem excessive, but it's a reasonable goal. Even a little is better than nothing. You may need to buy a pedometer, or download an app on your cell phone that will tell you how many steps you've taken. In addition to the cardiovascular benefits, regular walking delays the progression of knee arthritis, promotes mental clarity, and reduces depression.

Anaerobic exercise builds muscle strength. This can be done with the elaborate machines you find in a gym or with floor exercises and calisthenics at home.

Stretching all parts of your body should be a regular part of any workout.

Balance exercises are important because our balance deteriorates with age. This can be catastrophic if it leads to falls that cause broken hips or other fractures. Hip fractures usually require surgery and nursing home stays for rehab, and all too often they result in premature death. You can do a number of things to improve your balance. Dorothy and I practice by standing on one foot for the two-minute cycle of our electric toothbrushes each day.

After you've decided what your workout will include, the next step is to set up a schedule that helps you stay disciplined to exercise regularly. It won't be easy at first, but if you stick with it for two months, you'll find it becoming a habit. Stay with it longer, and you will see it turn into a good addiction.

Build up your strength and endurance, get control of your weight, and establish a pattern for the years to come. Be aware that many Medicare supplements, particularly Medicare Advantage programs, have the Silver Sneakers program, which includes a free gym membership to help you exercise faithfully.

Mental Health

Taking care of our bodies goes beyond our physical ability; we also need to do all we can to preserve our mental function.

Admittedly, some will develop dementia, where nerve death permanently damages parts of the brain. The bad news is that we cannot bring those nerves back to life.[2] Here we must trust that our powerful and loving God knows what's best for us, and that may include dementia.

The good news is that we may be able to strengthen the parts of the brain that aren't yet affected by dementia, simply by using them. This is no great secret—we need to use our brains. (I couldn't count how often my dad would say, "Johnny, just use your head.") It's not good enough to read or watch TV; we need to be actively engaged.

Personally, if I'm going to get something out of what I'm watching or reading, I need to write down my thoughts or talk to someone about them. This is particularly true in reading the Bible. Of course, there is spiritual value in just reading God's word. God may speak to us through it. But I find it more valuable to sit down with pen and paper, or nowadays with my computer, and record my thoughts. It also helps to talk to someone about what I'm reading.

We can also take on a hobby that requires us to think about what we're doing. Games can be great ways to exercise the brain. Dorothy and I know a lot of older couples who love to play games together. I'm not a game player, but Dorothy often tells me that we need to learn to play bridge if we want to get to know new couples, particularly those who aren't Christians.

2   For a fuller discussion of dementia, see my book *Finding Grace in the Face of Dementia* (Wheaton, IL: Crossway, 2017).

I've spoken of the value of recreation. Now I need to warn you of too much of something else—amusement (which at root literally means "no thinking"). It's true that at times our brains need a rest, and doing something that requires no thought can be re-creating. But too much amusement can devastate our brains. There's a lot of contemporary entertainment (including much of what's offered on TV) that is simply amusement and nothing more.

Curiosity is a wonderful attribute. When you were a kid, did you ever wonder how certain things worked? Why is the sky blue? What is a diesel engine? Now might be your opportunity to explore some of these questions and countless others. Go online or get to the local library and find some answers. Go to lectures, plays, and concerts; there may even be special programs and rates for seniors. Take others with you, particularly those who don't share your faith. Go out for dessert afterward, talk together about the performance, and critique the content from your different worldviews.

Now is your chance to explore new subjects. Consider taking some college courses. I recommend the Coursera website, where you'll find a vast number of courses from major universities that you can take.

Think about picking up the musical instrument you haven't touched since college, or consider learning a new one. Take up a new hobby, write an article or even a book, or do whatever you can to challenge your mind. There's no end of possibilities—so go ahead and expand your horizons.

Emotional Health

You also need to keep your emotional health strong. Start with some self-examination. Is your excitement about retirement mixed with a degree of depression? It frequently is for people. If so, the best solution is to recognize it for what it is. There are some simple steps you can take to help. Once you recognize it, the first step is to exercise. One study showed that a thirty-minute walk each day was in some cases as good for depression as medication.[3]

Second, be honest with God; learn to lament as you express how you truly feel inside. Third, have deeply caring friendships. Learn to laugh and cry with others. Be honest with people. When you're down, there's no reason to pretend that you're feeling great. If you're married, start by being honest with your spouse, and then with some good friends. God wants us to "bear one another's burdens" (Gal. 6:2). Note this is not a suggestion but fulfills the "law of Christ" (Gal. 6:2). Being honest and transparent will give others the privilege of bearing your burdens. At times, depression can be more severe and require medical help. I'll get to that in strategy 6.

One other way to preserve your emotional health after you retire is to avoid getting too busy. Over-busyness may be a temptation, but retirement should be exactly the opposite. Once you can slow down, treat yourself to a brief but refreshing nap, and now—perhaps for the first time in years—get sufficient sleep at night. Chances are, you'll be happier, feel better, and (counterintuitively) be more productive. Remember, our Lord commanded his people to have times for rest when he ordained a weekly Sabbath.

One day at the office I was running further behind than usual. I rushed into the examining room and was greeted by an elderly gentleman whom I knew quite well. He said, "Young man, you're

---

3 Patrick Barkham, "Is a Country Walk Better Than Prozac?," *The Guardian*, May 15, 2002, https://www.theguardian.com/lifeandstyle/.

late!" I immediately began to apologize. He interrupted me, proceeded to put his hands on my shoulders, sat me down on the exam table, and said, "Now, sit here for five minutes. Don't say or do anything. Slow down, and catch your breath." He then looked at his watch, and at the end of five minutes he said, "Okay, let's get going." It was an important lesson for me to learn.

As you recapture your physical, mental, and emotional strength (we'll get into spiritual strength next, in strategy 5), you'll find your energy levels and mental sharpness improve, and that will equip you to better enjoy retirement and your relationship with God, and to serve him better as well.

Questions to Ponder

1. In what ways do you need to get in shape physically, mentally, and emotionally?

2. Do you need to see your health-care professional or a physical trainer?

3. Do you "know your numbers"?

4. What steps can you take to keep learning and using your brain?

5. In light of what we've discussed for this strategy of taking care of yourself, what changes are you committed to making in your life?

PRAYER

Father, I know you expect me to be a good steward and to take care of the body and mind you've entrusted to me. I don't want my retirement to be cut short because I haven't taken care of myself. I need your help to know how to go about providing for my physical, mental, and emotional well-being and to have the discipline to stick to it.

I pray this for my good and your glory. Amen.

Love God

REMEMBER THAT THE FIRST instrumental way to glorify God is to love him "with all your heart and with all your soul and with all your mind" (Matt. 22:37).

Part of being human is to desire to love and be loved. Genuine love is a delight—never something onerous. We enjoy spending time with those we love, we think about the beauty of their character and person, and we want to know them better. So it is that loving God with a passion for his glory will prompt us to desire more time with him and to know him better. We'll identify with these heart-expressions from the Psalms:

> O God, you are my God; earnestly I seek you;
>   my soul thirsts for you;
> my flesh faints for you,
>   as in a dry and weary land where there is no water.
> So I have looked upon you in the sanctuary,
>   beholding your power and glory.
> Because your steadfast love is better than life,
>   my lips will praise you.

So I will bless you as long as I live;
in your name I will lift up my hands. (Ps. 63:1–4)

As a deer pants for flowing streams,
so pants my soul for you, O God.
My soul thirsts for God,
for the living God.
When shall I come and appear before God? (Ps. 42:1–2)

Perhaps you've recognized that your years of work haven't allowed you enough time to enjoy God. This has put your life out of balance. Now you need to make up for lost time. Your richer time with him will take two basic forms: hearing from him as you read, study, and meditate on the Bible, and communicating with him in prayer. As you come to know your all-powerful and wise Creator and Redeemer, you'll naturally love and enjoy him with an intensity that transcends all other loves, and you will long to see him glorified. What a joy it is to experience God in such deep and satisfying ways!

Now you can slow down, take ample time with the Lord, develop new ways to connect with him, and rekindle your relationship with him. It's such a high priority that I believe you need to set aside a generous amount of time for it each day when you first retire, even as you catch up on necessary things you've been putting off. Having more time to enjoy the Lord will go a long way in helping you recapture the balance in life you've been missing.

But the amazing thing is that while you've been deficient in time with God, he has missed his time with you. We must remember that he loves us, and we—as those he's purchased with his life—are his joy and delight. As David prayed, "I know that you delight in me" (Ps. 41:11). Consider these passages:

As the bridegroom rejoices over the bride,
    so shall your God rejoice over you. (Isa. 62:5)

The LORD your God is in your midst,
    a mighty one who will save;
he will rejoice over you with gladness;
    he will quiet you by his love;
he will exult over you with loud singing. (Zeph. 3:17)

The Lord invites us to come to him:

Come to me, all who labor and are heavy laden, and I will give you rest. Take my yoke upon you, and learn from me, for I am gentle and lowly in heart, and you will find rest for your souls. For my yoke is easy, and my burden is light. (Matt. 11:28–30)

Come, everyone who thirsts,
    come to the waters;
and he who has no money,
    come, buy and eat!
Come, buy wine and milk
    without money and without price. (Isa. 55:1)

Behold, I stand at the door and knock. If anyone hears my voice and opens the door, I will come in to him and eat with him, and he with me. (Rev. 3:20)

In Luke 15, Jesus tells of the great joy experienced when a lost sheep, a lost coin, and a lost son are recovered. All three of these stories speak of the joy God has when we—who have been too busy to have quality time with him—choose to reengage and draw closer to him.

A Sabbatical for Rest and Refocus

If we're going to recapture sweet time each day with the Lord, it will require significant change. This kind of change doesn't happen automatically or immediately. In his excellent book *An Uncommon Guide to Retirement*, Jeff Haanen emphasizes how God rested upon completing his work of creation, and in his law made provision for a weekly Sabbath and for festivals throughout the year. One year in every seven and two years out of every fifty were to be given over to the Lord.[1] Similarly we, too, need rest to regain our focus.

It may take a while to reprogram yourself, slow down in God's presence, and begin to have truly meaningful times with him. Feel free to take as much time as you need—weeks, months, even a year. Call it your sabbatical. Don't set a time limit on it. How long isn't important. Sure, you want to get back to a productive life of service, but remember how short you've been in time spent with the Lord and in your other priorities. Don't feel bad about not immediately jumping into other activities.

In the first days of this sabbatical you could plan for a spiritual retreat where you pull away completely from the busyness of life. When I left full-time practice, I took a three-day retreat. I walked, prayed, and paused frequently to read. I read many of my favorite psalms and scriptures. I was able to read much of J. I. Packer's *Knowing God*, then finished it over the next week or so. I wanted to recapture my first love for Jesus. I needed to slow down to rediscover the thrilling wonder and

---

1   Jeff Haanen, *An Uncommon Guide to Retirement: Finding God's Purpose for the Next Season of Life* (Chicago: Moody, 2019), 33–52.

beauty of my Savior. It was necessary to be quiet and hear his invitation to me: "Arise, my love, my beautiful one, and come away" (Song 2:10).

Jesus knows our need for this renewal, so when the disciples were exhausted and needed time for refreshment, he told them, "Come away by yourselves to a desolate place and rest a while" (Mark 6:31). My three-day retreat was enough to allow me to begin to live without the adrenaline. It was delightful, and afterward I felt ready to continue my longer sabbatical.

The first project in our sabbatical is to decide how to spend daily time with the Lord. This is our opportunity to break a habit many of us have—to quickly read a small portion of Scripture and offer a brief prayer each morning. Instead, we can retreat and meet more deeply with God every day.

Now you can relax, take time, and find a quiet place to be your sanctuary, where you read your Bible slowly, pause, and meditate. Then write some notes reflecting on what you learn and how you'll apply it. If you're a morning person, do this when you first get up. If you're an evening person, make sure you prioritize time with the Lord before bed.

Once you find a method that's comfortable and profitable for you, discipline yourself to spend time with the Lord every day till it becomes a habit. After more time, this can become another one of those good addictions you're unwilling to go without.

This time with the Lord will begin transforming you to be more like Jesus (2 Cor. 3:18). No longer simply maintaining your spiritual life, you will grow to think more like Jesus and respond to others as he would. Hopefully, these new spiritual habits will continue for as many years as God allows.

The sabbatical, while primarily intended to reinvigorate our loving relationship with the Lord, also allows us to review other priorities and to see where they'll fit in our retirement. These priorities include many of the strategies discussed in this book.

The goal of this sabbatical is to start retirement living according to your God-given priorities, and to establish life balance. A sabbatical also provides time to explore what activities you'll get involved in once you get back into a productive life as set out in your various strategies. For example, you may want to investigate ways you can serve in your church, a local homeless shelter, your library, or your park district.

Spiritual Disciplines

You've probably heard of the spiritual disciplines, and how saints of the past attested to the benefits they experienced in their own spiritual lives through these various practices. Perhaps you've dabbled with some of them, but have never been able to incorporate them regularly into your schedule. Retirement may be the time to reconsider them.

You can find various lists of different disciplines,. If you're intrigued, I suggest two classic books: Richard J. Foster's *Celebration of Discipline* and Dallas Willard's *The Spirit of the Disciplines*.[2] Practicing these disciplines should never be a legalistic obligation; rather, they should be an occasion for joy rooted in the Lord. They're another means whereby God, by his Spirit, can transform your character to be more like Jesus. God may also use them to help purify you and free you from sin, as you develop a love for God that exposes the lesser worth of the things and values of this world.

Here are some of the disciplines to consider.

2 Richard J. Foster, *Celebration of Discipline: The Path to Spiritual Growth* (San Francisco: Harper, 1978), and Dallas Willard, *The Spirit of the Disciplines: Understanding How God Changes Lives* (New York: Harper Collins, 1988).

Bible Reading and Study

This is likely the one discipline you already practice to some degree—and that's great! But perhaps it has become more mundane than meaningful. Do you ever find that after you've read a passage, you can't even say what it was about, let alone actually having allowed God to speak to you through it? I have. It helps to add two distinct elements to your reading: study and meditation.

First, study. Go through the text slowly to analyze it and make sure you understand what it's saying. If you read something you don't understand, take time to look it up in a commentary, study Bible, or Bible dictionary. Write out as many of your own observations on the text as you can.

On my first day in high school chemistry we were given candles and had thirty minutes to write down as many things about the candle as we could. It was amazing how many things we could observe. It was a good exercise to hone our abilities of observation. Similarly, we need to learn to carefully observe the Scriptures.

One lecture for beginning Yale medical students is taught in an art museum; it is titled "Looking Is Not Seeing." A companion lecture—"Listening Is Not Hearing"—is taught by the chair of the music department. Good medicine requires careful and detailed observation, without which many clues to the patient's problems will be missed. So it is in reading Scripture. Without careful and patient observation, we'll miss a lot of what God has to say.

My own practice is to import the full text of the book of the Bible I'm reading into my computer's word processor. Then I type in my own thoughts and observations between each verse, using the word processor's tracking function. After dealing with the text on my own, I look at the notes in a study Bible or in a commentary written on a nontechnical level. This gives me better understanding.

Some will benefit from a more formal study of the Scriptures. Your local church might offer courses that can provide more disciplined study. You can also check out offerings from a local seminary or Christian college or university. Explore courses you can audit or take for academic credit. Many of these resources are also available online.

Meditation

In addition to reading and studying the Scriptures, we must meditate on what we read. Note the promises given to someone who does this:

> His delight is in the law of the LORD,
>   and on his law he meditates day and night.
> He is like a tree
>   planted by streams of water
> that yields its fruit in its season,
>   and its leaf does not wither.
> In all that he does, he prospers. (Ps. 1:2–3)

It's wonderful to be able to clear our minds of other thoughts, and then turn to the Holy Spirit, asking him to control our thinking and lead us to meditate on the passage we've been reading. He may also lead us to go beyond that specific passage and meditate on larger themes throughout Scripture, such as the wonders and glories of God and his wisdom and power as revealed in creation (Ps.19) and as revealed in Jesus, the living Word. Marvel at the fact that Jesus came to earth to suffer and die to pay the penalty you owed to God because of your sin. Be thrilled that your salvation has opened the door for the Holy Spirit to come into your life. Then pray that God will lead you to think in these ways: "Finally, brothers, whatever is true, whatever is honorable, whatever is just, whatever is pure, whatever is lovely, whatever is commendable, if there is any excellence, if there is anything worthy of praise, think about these things" (Phil. 4:8).

Having time to meditate like this may well be one of your richest opportunities in retirement.

Reading Christian Literature

We can learn a lot from others, both our contemporaries and those from earlier generations. Retirement offers time to read; if reading is a problem, many audiobooks are available to listen to.

Read the church fathers and the Reformation giants like Augustine, Martin Luther, or John Calvin. Dig into the Puritans, such as John Owen, Richard Baxter, John Bunyan, and Jonathan Edwards. Spend time also in biographies, particularly of missionaries. Then get into some contemporary works. Find out which of your friends or pastors are voracious readers, and ask them for recommendations for what you should read.

In recent years, Dorothy and I have expanded our reading by getting podcasts, sermons, or full books on our phones. We listen to these while we walk, exercise, or work around the house. We seldom go anywhere without also having something to read or listen to.

Many local libraries have extensive online collections of downloadable electronic books and audiobooks. Your local library can give you free access to several sites. We enjoy the streaming apps Hoopla (which has an impressive number of Christian titles), Libby, and Overdrive.

Prayer

Now is the time to get serious and develop a robust prayer life. The old hymn "Sweet Hour of Prayer" may actually mean a full hour to you.

Even though we've been praying most of our lives, we still have a lot to learn about prayer. The disciples had likely been praying long before they met Jesus, yet they asked him, "Teach us to pray" (Luke 11:1).

In structuring my prayer, I like to use the acronym ACTS: Adoration, Confession, Thanksgiving, Supplication.

Adoration. Start with worshipful adoration where you express your love for God and your thrill over what he has revealed to us about himself. Take time to worship him for his great acts in creation and redemption. Our small group recently spent an evening reading and praying through Psalm 19. Every verse gave us a reason to adore God.

Confession. Adoring the holiness of God will show us our sin and unworthiness. Having more free time in retirement may lead to more sins of commission (things we do), but also provide time to recognize more sins of omission (things we fail to do). It's critical to confess all those sins and maintain a clean slate with God. Confession should always lead to repentance. This requires both an intentional turning away from sin and developing a specific plan to help ensure you won't repeat it. Confession should be followed by asking God to transform us from within, and to keep us from future sin:

> Create in me a clean heart, O God,
>   and renew a right spirit within me.
> Cast me not away from your presence,

and take not your Holy Spirit from me.
Restore to me the joy of your salvation,
    and uphold me with a willing spirit. (Ps. 51:10–12)

Thanksgiving. Cultivate a thankful heart. After confession, pause to be thankful for the forgiveness the Lord gives. This will circle us back to adoration of God. We should have a daily time to be thankful for recent blessings, but we must also periodically set aside an extended time to review our lives and thank God for what he has done in the past. Thank him for his grace in saving us, and for the mentors and experiences he has brought into our lives that have molded us and allowed our spiritual growth. God in his wisdom and love wants us to be "giving thanks always and for everything" (Eph. 5:20).

Supplication. After adoration, confession, and thanksgiving, there comes the appropriate time to make requests. God has asked us to bring our requests to him in faith, which means trusting him to do what's right. Don't limit your requests to a list of things you want to get. God wants to bless you in so many other ways! Review the prayers of Paul, and appreciate how he so frequently prayed for God to be glorified and for people to be transformed, rather than simply asking for specific things.[3]

If you're serious about prayer, it's wise to organize your prayer life. You could set aside a time each day to pray, and then focus on specific areas of need on each day of the week (as did my heroes I told you about in the introduction). This type of discipline will ensure that you go through your prayer list regularly. It may also help to start a prayer journal you can continually update as new needs arise and earlier requests are answered.

3   See also D. A. Carson, *Praying with Paul: A Call to Spiritual Reformation* (Grand Rapids, MI: Baker, 2014).

Fasting

The Bible talks a lot about fasting. These references concern abstaining from food, but fasting may also mean abstaining from anything that exerts control over our desires. The goal is to find joy and fulfillment more in God than in lesser things. In fasting we're essentially saying, "I don't need _____, because God is enough to satisfy me."

Some may want to fast on a regular schedule. And how long we fast is a highly individual matter. I've known people to fast by skipping only one meal, and others who choose to have only juices for forty days.

Calm and Quiet

Even in retirement, our lives can get so hectic that it's hard to focus on God. That was certainly my experience when working. I would get excited about doing something, and the adrenaline would start flowing. It was common to be so taken up with grand plans—some even geared toward God and his glory—that at times I was too busy to simply delight in God. In all honesty, I was too focused on myself and what I was doing.

Retirement can be the time to humble ourselves by letting go of those grand plans and finding contentment not in what we're doing but in what God has done. We all need to quit the busyness of our own agenda and learn to calm and quiet our souls, as David did:

O Lord, my heart is not lifted up;
    my eyes are not raised too high;
I do not occupy myself with things
    too great and too marvelous for me.

But I have calmed and quieted my soul,
    like a weaned child with its mother;
    like a weaned child is my soul within me. (Ps. 131:1–2)

To quiet your own soul, go where you can be alone with no interruptions. Find your contentment and satisfaction in Jesus; stop looking for it in other places. Jesus is enough. Keep reminding yourself of that. Rest and enjoy him.

Allow these passages to encourage and challenge you:

I wait for the LORD, my soul waits,
    and in his word I hope. (Ps. 130:5)

For God alone, O my soul, wait in silence,
    for my hope is from him. (Ps. 62:5)

Wait for the LORD;
    be strong, and let your heart take courage;
    wait for the LORD! (Ps. 27:14)

Lead me in your truth and teach me,
    for you are the God of my salvation;
    for you I wait all the day long. (Ps. 25:5)

"The LORD is my portion," says my soul,
    "therefore I will hope in him."
The LORD is good to those who wait for him,
    to the soul who seeks him. (Lam. 3:24–25)

Being quiet and resting in the Lord will then invigorate you to live for him:

But they who wait for the LORD shall renew their
strength;
they shall mount up with wings like eagles;
they shall run and not be weary;
they shall walk and not faint. (Isa. 40:31)

Simplicity

Isn't it amazing how much stuff we accumulate over the years? We spoke in strategy 3 of the value of eliminating some of the clutter we've built up over the years. Material things can become a burden, as well as objects of our affection that distract us from our ability to enjoy God. Some possessions are indeed a cause of sinful pride. We easily enjoy showing off our homes and cars because we're proud of them. But remember the words of Jesus:

> Do not lay up for yourselves treasures on earth, where moth and rust destroy and where thieves break in and steal, but lay up for yourselves treasures in heaven, where neither moth nor rust destroys and where thieves do not break in and steal. For where your treasure is, there your heart will be also. (Matt. 6:19–21)

Dorothy and I were impressed when, over the years, her widowed mother first sold her family home and bought a smaller condo, then moved to an even smaller apartment, then later move to a single room in an assisted-living facility. To take each step, she would have a yard sale to divest herself of "things" and regain some capital.

Downsizing and ridding ourselves of accumulated things can allow for the next discipline, generosity.

Generosity

Many people spend their working years building up a retirement nest egg. Some have been so blessed financially that there's more than enough money for even a worst-case scenario. Now is the time for the spiritual discipline of generosity.

Learn the joy of giving and honoring God by returning to him some of what he has so generously given to you. To those who are "rich in this present age," here is Paul's instruction: "They are to do good, to be rich in good works, to be generous and ready to share" (1 Tim. 6:17–18). Jesus said, "It is more blessed to give than to receive" (Acts 20:35).

A good estate plan can allow you to be generous after you die, when your funds no longer need to be kept in reserve. But you can also be generous now, while you're still alive and able to see your funds contribute to the work of God's kingdom today. As you consider where to distribute funds that you don't envision needing during your lifetime, remember that your children and grandchildren may have more need now for help with education and housing than after you die. You may also want to fund good memories for the family. Take the entire family on a trip, or do other things they'll remember and cherish after you're gone.

This is also the time to be more conscious of the financial needs of the poor around you, and to investigate ways you can truly help them without creating a situation where they become dependent or lose self-respect.

Another aspect of generosity is hospitality. What a joy to share your home, food, and other comforts with others! The command of Scripture is clear: "Show hospitality to one another" (1 Pet. 4:9). I've seen many seniors excel at this. Whether you invite people in for a meal or entertain guests overnight, this is a great way to serve God and to broaden your horizons.

Celebration

This is a spiritual discipline that's less commonly named as such, but one that we must practice. God tells us to rejoice. Our church's worship services are certainly appropriate times to celebrate, but there are many other occasions to celebrate what God does for us.

> Make a joyful noise to the LORD, all the earth!
>> Serve the LORD with gladness!
>> Come into his presence with singing!
> Know that the LORD, he is God!
>> It is he who made us, and we are his;
>> we are his people, and the sheep of his pasture.
> Enter his gates with thanksgiving,
>> and his courts with praise!
>> Give thanks to him; bless his name!
> For the LORD is good;
>> his steadfast love endures forever,
>> and his faithfulness to all generations. (Ps. 100)

Lament

Wonderful times of celebration must be balanced by lament. We need to honestly cry out to God when we're hurting. We need to be able to feel deeply the difficulties of life both for ourselves and for others—and as we do, we must cry out to God for his help.

So many of the psalms are laments. Psalm 13 begins with this plaintive cry:

How long, O LORD? Will you forget me forever?
　　How long will you hide your face from me?
How long must I take counsel in my soul
　　and have sorrow in my heart all the day?
How long shall my enemy be exalted over me?
　　　(Ps. 13:1–2)

There's nothing spiritual about denying the pain and disappointment we feel. Even while we lament, we can continue to trust God. As David wrote, "I cry out to God Most High, to God who fulfills his purpose for me" (Ps. 57:2).

———

Each of these disciplines is worth considering, and knowing how to practice them in retirement may be challenging. But don't assume you must think through these things entirely on your own. Sit down with your pastor and get some advice. Talk to your spouse or others who know you well. Probe the experiences of spiritually mature friends who have already retired, and discover how they're practicing these disciplines.

The Local Church

Whatever other activities we're involved in, we must allow a role for the local church. We must appreciate the value God places on the church: "Christ loved the church and gave himself up for her" (Eph. 5:25). Paul eloquently expresses the importance of the church by calling it "the fullness of him who fills all in all" (Eph. 1:23).

In light of these truths, it would be hard to dispute the importance of the universal church or its local congregations. At all stages of life, we need to have corporate worship, prayer, teaching from the Scriptures, pastoral care, fellowship, and accountability.

The truth is that the older we are, the more difficult it is to become established in a local church. This is a major argument for moving to what you feel will be your final destination while still relatively young and able to make a contribution in a church.

In all stages of life, we must in some way serve the church. And there will come times when we'll need the humility to give the church the privilege of serving us.

Spiritual Gifts

Scripture teaches that all believers are given specific abilities to benefit their local congregation. These are called spiritual gifts.

In 1 Corinthians 12, Paul gives extensive teaching on these gifts. He instructs us that gifts are given to every believer (no exceptions) for the benefit of the common good. Impressively, there are no age limitations. Even a ninety-year-old believer will have some way in which the Holy Spirit can use him or her to benefit the church.

The New Testament provides a number of lists that give examples of these gifts. There's no reason to assume that even the composite of all these lists is exhaustive. Nor should we assume that any individual will have the same gift throughout his or her life. As we get older, our strength and natural abilities will change. As they do, the Holy Spirit may bless our local congregation by gifting us in different ways. So, as the years go by, we need to be flexible in how we serve. For example, in my younger years I felt quite comfortable doing administrative activities. Now there are many younger people who are more capable than I at this, so I want them to take over.

My observation has been that older retirees are often especially gifted in two particular ways: praying for others and encouraging others.

Spiritual Growth

God, by his Spirit, is transforming our characters to be more like Jesus: "And we all, with unveiled face, beholding the glory of the Lord, are being transformed into the same image from one degree of glory to another. For this comes from the Lord who is the Spirit" (2 Cor. 3:18).

We were made in the image of God; our character is to reflect God in various ways. We do so imperfectly, but the Holy Spirit works in us to transform us to gradually reflect him more. One of our goals should be to increasingly reflect that image more perfectly until the time he calls us to himself.[4]

One way the Holy Spirit works this transformation is by giving us what Scripture calls the fruit of the Spirit: "The fruit of the Spirit is love, joy, peace, patience, kindness, goodness, faithfulness, gentleness, self-control; against such things there is no law" (Gal. 5:22–24). This fruit is to become so deeply ingrained in our character that it will determine our default responses.

I'm intrigued how various natural fruits come in different seasons: strawberries in the spring, blueberries and peaches in the summer, apples in the fall. Likewise, the fruit of the Spirit in different forms may develop in us in different seasons of our lives. For many of us, gentleness and patience tend to be more late-blooming fruits. As we progress through our years of retirement, we're wise to periodically assess our progress in displaying this fruit.

The apostle Peter tells us to grow "in grace and knowledge" (2 Pet. 3:18). Growing in grace requires a better understanding of how unworthy we are of God's favor, and also how dependent we are on this grace. It also requires us to be more gracious

---

4 To better understand the image of God, I recommend John Kilner's excellent *Dignity and Destiny: Humanity in the Image of God* (Grand Rapids, MI: Eerdmans, 2015).

toward others. Meanwhile, growth in knowledge requires us to more deeply understand basic truths about Jesus—who he is as the God-man, his life, death, and resurrection, and his offer of salvation to those who believe in him.

All this growth occurs even during the time of life when many of us will find our mental capabilities deteriorating, especially if we're experiencing some degree of dementia. In that situation, we must continuously review and be reminded of the basic tenets of our faith.[5]

Though many of us have to some degree neglected our love for God during our working years, retirement is the time to turn that around. This is best done early in our retirement, and may require time for us to pull away from the busyness of life and to begin developing new habits of spiritual devotion, before we fill our retirement years with less important things.

Questions to Ponder

1. Would you agree that the greatest lack in your working years has been your daily time with your Lord?

2. How do you respond to the suggestion of taking a sabbatical? How should you go about it? How long do you think it will take for you to rebuild your spiritual life and form new habits?

3. Which of the spiritual disciplines do you especially want to start practicing now?

5   For more on this sensitive topic, see Benjamin Mast's *Second Forgetting: Remembering the Power of the Gospel during Alzheimer's Disease* (Grand Rapids, MI: Zondervan, 2014).

4. How do you see your spiritual gifts changing?

5. In what areas do you need to grow spiritually?

6. In light of what we've discussed about this strategy for loving God, what changes are you committed to make in your life?

PRAYER

Precious Lord, for all these years I've desired to draw closer to you, but for a variety of reasons I haven't been able to come as close as I've wanted. Now, in retirement, I sincerely want to do so, and I have no more excuses. I long to reach the end of my life walking closely with you, being fully satisfied with you, and finding you as my greatest joy. I know that this will glorify you—and that is my goal.

I need your help to show me how to deepen my time with you. How should I go about studying and meditating on your word? How should I construct my prayer life? Which of the spiritual disciplines should I practice? In what ways can I serve my church? Without your leading and help I will fail—so guide me.

I pray this for the sake of your glory, and I know it will prove to be for my good. Amen.

Make Good Friends

WORK HAS DEPRIVED many of us of the privilege to sit, relax, and enjoy unstructured time with good friends. This is another deficit we need to correct in retirement.

There are both solid science and the teaching of Scripture in support of our need for good friendships. Scientifically it has been shown that people who maintain strong social connections live longer and happier lives than those who are more isolated.[1] Scripture tells us, "It is not good that the man should be alone" (Gen. 2:18). Though written in the context of marriage, it's also true on a much broader level. We were created with the need to be in community rather than be lone rangers. In eternity past before time began, our triune God demonstrated loving relationships within the Godhead.

Friendships open new worlds for us, allow us the joy of serving others, and open opportunities to share the good news of Jesus with those who do not yet know him.

---

1   See for example "Friends and Longevity: The Science of Social Connection," *Health-Guide* website, April 8, 2020, https://www.getroman.com/health-guide/friends-and -longevity/.

Expand Your Circle of Friends

One of the unfortunate realities of retirement is that it often involves the loss of close friends. As we discussed in strategy 2, these are likely people you've built very comfortable relationships with over time, and you feel more natural in sharing your life with them. They know your faith, respect you for it, and allow you to discuss it naturally with them.

Despite our good intentions, once we lose the common bond of work, we tend to grow apart from these friends, and such close friends are hard to replace. Once you retire, it may be some time before you can build similarly close friendships, whether with Christians or not. It will require determined effort.

Another reality is that during the years of retirement, your social group will continually change. Over time many of your friends will move away, and some will die. Others will develop medical problems that limit their ability to enjoy the activities you've done together in the past; this doesn't mean they won't continue to be friends, but how you spend your time together will change. The result is that you'll need to continually make new friends.

Moreover, as time goes on you may find it harder to meet new people and to build friendships. You may not get out as often with new people. Many find that with age, not only their bodies and minds but also their social skills get rusty. You may feel embarrassed about not remembering names or what people told you about themselves. Making friends may become challenging enough that you stop trying.

If you're feeling lonely and in need of a friend, but finding it difficult to make one, it's helpful to realize that plenty of others around you are experiencing the same frustration. Like you, they may be hoping someone will reach out and want to be their friend.

Remember that one of the best ways to cultivate friendship is learning to listen. Let others tell their story. Ask probing questions that show your interest and demonstrate that you've been listening, but otherwise don't interrupt or talk too much about yourself. Listen for things you can do to help them in practical ways. Remember that Jesus came "not to be served but to serve" (Mark 10:45).

If you want to make a friend with someone you've just met, slow down and enjoy the present moment. Don't spend the time thinking about the past or what's coming down the line. Don't even think about what you'll say next. Allow yourself to laugh and enjoy the person. Over time, as the friendship grows, it's fine to be honest about what gives you joy and what frustrates you, but don't habitually complain.

If you're married, it's great to have several other couples that the two of you can do things with. But don't allow all your friendships to be couple to couple. Guys need to have guy friends, and women need to get out with other women. Not to sound morbid, but these friends will be invaluable support to you if your spouse dies.

Another way to expand your circle of friends is to reconnect with old friends. When I was in medical school, there was a group of five of us who were Christians out of the hundred in our class. We met once a week for Bible study and prayer for the first three years, and then before our final year we almost doubled the size of our group when four of us married. Over the years we maintained a "Christmas card" relationship, and then last year we all got together for a delightful fifty-year reunion. Reconnecting was a refreshing way to expand our friendships.

Kinds of Friends

Below are other kinds of friendships you can and should pursue.

Just for Fun

Some people are fun to spend time with. There's no need for any agenda or planned projects to do together; it's fine to just hang out and enjoy each other's company.

Chances are your working years didn't provide much opportunity for fun relationships like that. Even outside work, you were busy doing various projects with your friends. Your time together was spent talking about what you were doing rather than enjoying each other. Now, in retirement, you can release those projects and enjoy friends for who they are as people, not for the projects you can do together.

I learned a lot by observing my father. Dad was an entrepreneur. He started several businesses, was on several college and mission boards, helped plant three churches, and spearheaded the founding of a Christian radio station. He had many friends, but they were always involved together in various projects. After he retired, for the first time I saw him relax and spend time with others just for the sake of enjoying them. Was his earlier drive and productivity bad? I don't think so, but it was only after he slowed down to relax with others that he began to enjoy people more than projects.

Sharing a Common Interest

Some people have a hobby like golf or crafts that will give them a natural way to relax and enjoy spending time with others. Dorothy and I have always loved to take long walks together. We're increasingly encouraging others to join us. Everyone needs the exercise, and particularly in these days of the lingering COVID-19 pandemic, it's a much safer way to spend time with others.

Some who don't already have this kind of outlet will need to seek out new activities to build friendships. Perhaps you'll find friends at a health club, senior center, or a service or hobby club, or through volunteering at a hospital, library, or homeless shelter. Other options are taking a class at a local college or attending a public lecture series that meets often enough for you to connect with others. When you meet someone in one of these contexts, it immediately gives you a shared interest, providing reasons to get together in the future.

Christian Fellowship

Another category of friends are those with whom we can have Christian fellowship. This tends to be of two kinds. Some are relaxed and rather superficial, like sipping coffee together between services at church. I call that "fellow*sip*," and there's nothing wrong with it. But others are deep relationships where there's a transparency that allows us to share our deepest feelings and thoughts with each other. These often develop out of some service done together and the need to depend on each other. I refer to this in-depth fellowship as "two fellows on a ship."

We need both kinds of fellowship. The superficial fellow*sip* can be automatic. We must be very deliberate to cultivate the deeper two-fellows-on-a-ship model.

We are part of a wonderful small group through our church. We meet weekly through the year, share what's going on in our lives, take an hour to discuss and apply the previous week's sermon, and then break into smaller groups to pray for each other. We range in age from mid-twenties to mid-seventies. The socioeconomic spectrum runs from one couple formerly living in a homeless shelter to a university professor. Over time we've developed a deep love for each other, and we've moved into deep fellowship. Dorothy and I love the bond this gives us with people whose experience with Jesus has differed from our own. It's enriching and broadens our understanding.

Evangelism

With our newly balanced life allowing us to spend more time appreciating and loving Jesus, it's likely that our desire to share him with others will increase. There may have been many things about our work life that kept us from talking about Jesus. There may have been time constraints. Busyness was a big issue for many of us. For others it was a question of ethics; we didn't feel it was fair to use the time for which our employer was paying us to talk to coworkers about faith. Perhaps we held back from sharing our faith for fear it would destroy our reputation (this was likely due to our own pride).

Whatever they were, those reasons not to talk about Jesus are now gone. Our more relaxed lifestyle and ability to spend time to become closer friends with non-Christians may give us ways to serve them and increased opportunities to share our faith with them.

Friendships that will lead to opportunities for evangelism should be a feature of retirement, but the reality is that this will never happen if we sequester ourselves with Christians and do not, in some way, begin to spend time with non-Christians.

The ways we develop friendships with non-Christians are really no different from how we meet other friends. The difference is that when we place a priority on evangelism, we'll more deliberately engage our new friends in serious conversations and ask questions that will encourage them to think about the bigger issues of life. One of my good friends uses the sauna at his gym as his mission field. He has engaged the men who are regularly in the sauna in meaningful discussions so often that they now call him the chaplain of the sauna.

Some have the gift of evangelism and can approach a total stranger and start talking about Jesus and his need for the Savior. Others of us feel more comfortable meeting a non-Christian and getting to know him slowly by spending unhurried time together. As we begin to share more of our lives, it will be increasingly obvious that our faith is part of who we are. Our new friends may initially be intrigued, and soon they may be attracted to our faith and desire a relationship with Jesus.

Some shared activities may be more conducive to this. For example, watching a movie together or attending a lecture and then going out for dessert may lead to more evangelistic conversations than going to a ball game. Whatever we do, it's important that our friends have a good time. One of my friends frequently reminds me that the only thing we can take to heaven with us are our friends.

Diversity

The body of Christ is made up of all kinds of people, and if we allow a variety of Christians to impact our lives, we'll become more like Jesus. This is why I intentionally spend more time with believers from diverse national and ethnic backgrounds. It has been a wonderful experience.

I value not only ethnic diversity but also age diversity. It's a privilege to spend time with younger people. I especially love being with medical students. It's sweet to encourage them to think about Jesus and how he would relate to patients. I'm energized by them, and they sometimes express appreciation for perspectives I've shared with them.

I'm impressed that in today's world, Millennials and Generation Z are much more open to input from seniors than the average baby boomer of fifty years ago. This was evidenced rather dramatically when Dorothy and I were at church years ago, and a young lady who appeared to be in her midtwenties approached us and said, "You have gray hair, could I ask you a question?" No longer do we talk about the generation gap that was in vogue in the sixties.

Baby boomers like me shouldn't hesitate—out of fear of rejection—to reach out to younger people. For years I've used the term "mentoring" in speaking of my relationship with younger men. I realize now that this is the wrong terminology. Instead, I now talk about "intergenerational friendships," because that emphasizes not what I contribute to them but what we contribute to each other.

There's also a great advantage in socioeconomic diversity. I want to learn what it was like to grow up in poverty, needing to surmount the hurdles faced by those without the privilege and resources I was given as a child and young adult. I need to spend time with these brothers and sisters and allow them to teach me how I can help people who lack resources, and to do so in a way that won't create dependence or destroy their sense of dignity. I must ask how their poverty shaped their experience with God and what they can teach me about him.

In similar and frequently overlapping ways, there's value in educational diversity. Not all wisdom is learned by books and study. Much is gained from experience, and I can learn much from those who've been educated by the hard knocks of life. Those with more formal education need to benefit from diversity across various disciplines. Those in the sciences can learn from those in the humanities, and vice versa. I love to ask people from a totally different educational background what books I should read. Having had so much of my education in the sciences, I'm now reading some of the great literature of centuries past, and I'm enjoying it.

Finally, I appreciate diversity across the larger body of Christ. Dorothy and I, in our pursuit of diversity, currently worship in two churches. We attend an early morning service of a church that's historically black, and a later morning service at a church that's more international. We spend time with friends from both congregations; we love it and are enriched by them.

New Haven has an association called Bridges of Hope. Initially this organization was made up of eight gospel-preaching and Bible-teaching pastors who previously had hardly known each other. Starting in 2014, they spent a year building friendships among themselves. Now their churches sponsor community service projects together, pray for each other, and encourage friendships across congregational lines.

Through Bridges of Hope and other contacts, I have benefitted from friendships with Christians from many denominations, including Presbyterian, Episcopalian, Methodist, Catholic, and Pentecostal. With this diverse exposure, I've experienced Jesus in new and different ways, and hopefully I'm growing to be more like him.

Questions to Ponder

1. How are you going about making new friends?

2. How important to you is it to have friends who aren't Christian?

3. Are you able to slow down, relax, and simply enjoy being with someone, with no personal agenda of your own?

4. What value do you place on being exposed to ethnic diversity? Cultural diversity? Socioeconomic diversity? Educational diversity? Denominational diversity?

5. In light of what we've discussed for this strategy of making good friends, what changes are you committed to make in your life?

PRAYER

Heavenly Father, I know I need good friends. I pray that you'll help me value people for who they are, and not just as helpers to accomplish my own agenda. Lead me to people who need a friend and who need to know your forgiveness through Jesus. Give me a love for others so I can help and encourage them. I know this is one way to reflect your glory. Amen.

Enjoy and Strengthen Your Family

FOR THOSE WHO ENTER retirement blessed to be married and to have grown children and possibly grandchildren, retirement offers wonderful, God-given opportunities for joy, enrichment, and opportunities to serve. For those who are single, retirement provides more time to build close, satisfying relationships, some of which will become close long-term relationships. These platonic (not sexual) relationships become close to the equivalent of marriage and family. Many of the suggestions in this strategy will apply to these relationships, and not exclusively to marriage.

We've been talking about priorities and the key decisions we face. This includes determining how our marriage and family will fit into our retirement. How much time should we spend together as a couple? How much time should we devote to children and grandchildren? Will our interaction with family represent a significant way in which God is glorified?

Time with spouse and family is a gift from God to be treasured, and most people highly appreciate the value of this gift. One study showed that 40 percent of Americans consider spending time with family as their most important source of meaning and fulfillment, while 70 percent say that family gives their lives a "great deal" of meaning.[1]

Marriage

Having a clear picture of what a marriage in the later years should look like is essential to a good post-retirement marriage experience.[2] Recall Robert Browning's lines, "Grow old along with me! The best is yet to be."[3] Perhaps that's a bit idealistic, and yet the astute Christian counselor Paul Tournier also wrote glowingly of marriage in later life: "Growing old together, husband and wife can come to know a love which is in a way a prefiguration of heaven, for it is less tumultuous than the love of youth, being less directed toward selfish pleasure-seeking."[4]

Yes, retirement can be a profound blessing to a marriage when two people deeply in love with each other are longing for more time together, especially if they have resented living largely separate lives during their working days. But some marriages thrive by husband and wife being separated during the workday, then sitting down together for an evening meal and telling each other about their day. Other couples are able to happily work together most of the time—in the same office or store, for example.

It's important for retiring couples in these healthy marriages to discuss how their individual strengths can complement each other, now that they'll have more time together. The goal will

---

1 These percentages are reported by Lydia Dugdale in *The Lost Art of Dying: Reviving Forgotten Wisdom* (New York: HarperOne, 2020), 201.

2 This section, primarily written by my good friend Dr. Charles Sell, is largely taken from my book *Wellness for the Glory of God* (Wheaton, IL: Crossway, 2014).

3 These are the opening lines of Robert Browning's poem "Rabbi Ben Ezra," a meditation concerning a twelfth-century poet and philosopher, in Browning's *Dramatis Personae* (Boston, 1864).

4 Paul Tournier, *Learn to Grow Old*, trans. Edwin Hudson (New York: Harper & Row, 1972), 94.

be for them as a couple to accomplish more for God than the two of them could do separately. (Or as I often say, one plus one equals three.) To do this, they must learn to combine their individual strengths to compensate for their individual weaknesses. This requires a humble recognition of each other's strengths and shortcomings, and making a commitment not to compete with each other or dominate one another. Rather, they become the team God wants them to be, and they find activities that they both enjoy, and in which they work together well.

Dorothy and I thought a lot about our shared desire to retire soon enough to take on various activities together. We were intrigued to realize that though we had spent our working years in rather parallel ways in medicine, we had rarely done much together. Our prayers were that God would give us wisdom to choose a way we could serve him together. We recognized that if this were to work, we needed to retire at about the same time so that we could embark on our new service projects on an equal basis. I retired six months before her. I didn't want to get into new projects till we could do so together. Meanwhile, I needed something to keep me busy till she retired. Writing this book became my interim project.

A good, spiritually productive marriage after retirement is the ideal, but unfortunately it is not the default. The rich opportunities that marriage and family bring are not without their challenges. Some marriages have survived before retirement only because the husband and wife had ample time apart; their marriage foundation was shaky. When they're together, the little things that bug them about each other are magnified. More time together in retirement may become a threat to such marriages. These couples may be better off to continue functioning separately until they get counseling, attend marriage seminars, or do some helpful reading and talking together to learn ways to improve their marriage.

Marriages in retirement may face other sources of tension. The husband and wife may have had well-defined roles in the home, and now, as they start sharing the work, they interfere with each other. It's usually essential that the housework be divided equitably. If not, retirement won't provide any change or relief for the partner who previously has been doing most of the housework. And when a new role or responsibility is taken on, the spouse who's new at it may not do the job as well as it was done by the other spouse in the past. This may require talking through the issue to achieve mutual understanding.

Several additional lessons—many taught in Scripture—are relevant to marriage in our later years. These involve companionship, intimacy, and transformation.

Companionship

The Bible teaches that the fundamental nature of marriage is companionship. In Genesis 2:24 God refers to the marital bond as being "one flesh." That's not strictly a metaphor for sexual intercourse. Old Testament scholar Richard Averbeck observes:

> The point . . . is that the man will bond with the woman in permanent personal commitment that will never come apart. They become "one flesh" in the sense that they become one functional unit, dealing with life together in bond with one another.[5]

One aspect of companionship may allow time for couples to pursue spiritual growth and devotion together. By sharing in worship, prayer, and Bible study, the husband and wife can encourage each

---

5   Richard Averbeck, "Wisdom from the Old Testament," in *Why the Church Needs Bioethics: A Guide to Wise Engagement with Life's Challenges*, ed. John F. Kilner (Grand Rapids, MI: Zondervan, 2001), 38.

other to know God better and to allow the Spirit to invigorate their marriage.

Often, we think relating spiritually is done by doing some sort of "devotional" together. That's important for many couples, but some (including Dorothy and me) do better having separate times with the Lord, which we both treasure. However, we also enjoy sharing with each other from what we're learning. Over the years, our primary way to share together spiritually has been praying together.

Some of our most meaningful shared spiritual experiences occur informally and spontaneously. After watching a spectacular sunset, we can bow together and worship God for creating such beauty as well as giving us the capacity to enjoy it. After getting a phone call or text asking for prayer, we can stop and intercede together with the Lord. If we learn of an ongoing international crisis, we can pray for those involved. All this must surely be part of what the apostle Paul had in mind when he urged us to "pray without ceasing" (1 Thess. 5:17).

Intimacy

Marriage provides an opportunity to know and be known in the closest of all human relationships. In later life, with the children gone, a couple has more time to cultivate a closeness that was difficult in busier days. This allows for mutual sharing of inner feelings and private emotions, which in turn promotes intimacy. Unfortunately, some people shy away from sharing these feelings, for various reasons. It's important for them to try to risk more sharing.

Intimate companionship can be enhanced in many other ways, such as playing, working, praying, or serving together. Physical intimacy is always important. There should still be lots of hugs, kisses, and loving touch. This can also include sexual intercourse, if physical capacity and desire are present.

Intimacy on any level is God's intention to promote unity within marriage, and it serves as a guard against infidelity.

Transformation

God also uses marriage as a tool in his project to transform us to be more like Jesus. I often think of the Old Testament picture of the potter's wheel. In fact, hanging above the area where I write is an etching of a potter at his wheel; it was done by an artist friend many years ago. The lesson from it for me is clear: while I may not willingly volunteer to be plopped down on a wheel, spun around at five hundred rpms, and have all my rough edges knocked off, that's exactly what God is doing for me.

Like it or not, God often uses my marriage as the potter's wheel to transform me—and that's okay, for who could I trust more than my loving heavenly Father to be the potter? The finished product (when I get to heaven) will be wonderful, even though the process may not be fun at the moment.

Give Each Other Space

Don't try to be together too much. It may help to set aside places in your home for each other to have some alone time. Plan some activities that are his, some that are hers, and others shared by both. Men need to have some men they spend time with, and women need other women. If you do some things separately, you'll likely enjoy doing more things together.

Recognize That Any Marriage Is Fragile

Be kind and considerate to each other. Share the work equitably. Be careful in your speech. James tells us, "Let every person be quick to hear, slow to speak, slow to anger; for the anger of man does not produce the righteousness of God" (James 1:19–20). This is particularly relevant when you start spending a lot of time together.

If your marriage is beginning to feel shaky, recognize this, and talk and pray about it together. If necessary, seek counseling, and make the necessary adjustments.

Prepare Together for the Future

We've discussed many of the positive things we can do in retirement to enrich a marriage, but we must not overlook our responsibility to prepare each other for the undeniable fact that one spouse will likely die before the other. It's imperative that this be carefully talked through.

The surviving spouse needs to be able to take over the responsibilities performed routinely by the other. Both need to understand their finances, how to cook, clean the house, and take care of the car. Both need to have living wills and understand the nature of the medical care they want individually in view of life-threatening illness. They need to know each other's preferences about a funeral or memorial service, and about burial or cremation. It's also important to discuss these issues not only with your spouse but with your children as well. These things are never easy to discuss, but it's a necessary part of growing old together.

Children

Hopefully, by God's grace, your children are living independent, responsible lives. They've been launched like an arrow into their own lives.

> Behold, children are a heritage from the LORD,
>   the fruit of the womb a reward.

Like arrows in the hand of a warrior
    are the children of one's youth. (Ps. 127:3–4)

We're not primarily responsible for our grown children, but we must always be available to them to talk over issues they're facing. This necessitates intentional time to talk together as adults.

Consider these instructions from Deuteronomy as the responsibility of a father to instruct his children:

> Hear, O Israel: The LORD our God, the LORD is one. You shall love the LORD your God with all your heart and with all your soul and with all your might. And these words that I command you today shall be on your heart. You shall teach them diligently to your children, and shall talk of them when you sit in your house, and when you walk by the way, and when you lie down, and when you rise. (Deut. 6:4–7)

Though we typically apply this passage to rearing small children, we should note that the text doesn't say anything about age. The Hebrew word translated here as "children" could be applied to children of any age.

Our children are typically adults when we retire, and it's in their adulthood that they perhaps need to be reminded most of the requirement to have only one God and to love him with their whole being. We might need to have frequent discussions with them about God and his proper role in our lives. Too often during the busyness of our working years, when our children are teenagers and young adults, these conversations have been ignored, and our relationships may have been strained. Retirement may offer the opportunity to correct that.

Our relationship with our adult children will be different than when they were younger, since they're no longer under our authority. We'll be blessed not only to benefit from their friendship but from their wisdom. Our roles will continue to shift, and we may be less the givers and more the receivers. As we get closer to the end of our lives, it's even more important to cultivate and treasure our relationship with our children.

The psalmist had this as one of his goals in his later years:

> So even to old age and gray hairs,
>   O God, do not forsake me,
> until I proclaim your might to another generation,
>   your power to all those to come. (Ps. 71:18)

Our children have likely already heard us talk about God's righteousness, power, and the great things he has done. Still, we need to retell those stories so they can be passed on by our children to future generations. This ongoing continuity from one generation to the next is part of God's eternal plan, as we see in Psalm 78:

> He established a testimony in Jacob
>   and appointed a law in Israel,
> which he commanded our fathers
> to teach to their children,
>   that the next generation might know them,
> the children yet unborn,
>   and arise and tell them to their children,
> so that they should set their hope in God
>   and not forget the works of God,
> but keep his commandments. (Ps. 78:5–7)

In addition to passing on the basic stories of the Bible, we need to share with our children about times in our lives when we've experienced God in particularly dramatic ways. We shouldn't tell these stories as if we were the hero. God is the hero. In addition to the good stories, we must tell of the difficult times when we failed, and the lessons we learned.

This can apply in our relationship not only to biological children but also to other younger people in whose lives we're involved. This is one of the reasons we need to maintain friendships across generations. This may include neighbors, church friends, and even friends of our children. Age-based segregation that continually sets seniors apart from the younger generations, whether in a church or the broader community, can be devastating to both. Seniors need the energy, clear thinking, fresh perspectives, humor, and enthusiasm of those who are younger, while younger persons need the experience, wisdom, maturity, and example of faithfulness that they see in seniors.

Grandchildren

The Bible speaks more of the role of grandparents than we often recognize. It usually doesn't speak of grandchildren or grandparents, but more often uses phrases like "children's children" or "future generations," so this teaching is easy to overlook.

In today's world, many seniors will see not only their grandchildren but also their great-grandchildren. This hasn't always been so. One interesting statistic is that in 1850, an average woman only lived for one year after her youngest child married. With current longevity rates, most of us have the privilege to be increasingly involved in the lives of our grandchildren. Grandparents today tend to be healthier and more active than in prior generations. This is a great privilege, but as with any privilege, we must be good stewards of these God-given opportunities. It's sad that our culture tends to see grandparents as uninvolved with grandchildren, or simply as babysitters, playmates, or companions.

In truth, grandparents can contribute to the lives of their grandchildren in many meaningful ways. Consider being fellow learners. Talk together about things you would both like to learn more about and then go online or to the library to learn together.

Wouldn't it be wonderful if you could help them grow in their relationship with God? You would become the disciple-making grandparent we'll consider shortly. What a rich opportunity this can be for retired grandparents! One of my enduring memories is of my godly grandmother continually reminding me of God's promise that "those who honor me I will honor" (1 Sam. 2:30).

An impactful relationship between grandparents and their grandchildren requires a close working partnership between the grandparents and their own children, along with sufficient time (often meaning close enough distance) for grandparents to be with their grandchildren. This may force us to rethink a choice to move away from our grandchildren.

Biblical Grandparenting

In his book *Biblical Grandparenting: Exploring God's Design for Disciple-Making and Passing Faith to Future Generations*, Josh Mulvihill makes several excellent, biblically based points that I take the liberty to summarize.[6]

1. Grandchildren are evidence of God's blessing.

---

6 Josh Mulvihill, *Biblical Grandparenting: Exploring God's Design for Disciple-Making and Passing Faith to Future Generations* (Minneapolis: Bethany House, 2018).

The LORD bless you from Zion!
  May you see the prosperity of Jerusalem
  all the days of your life!
May you see your children's children! (Ps. 128:5–6)

Grandchildren are the crown of the aged. (Prov. 17:6)

2. We must talk to our grandchildren about God frequently. God can use us as a means for them to come to faith, learn to fear him, and do what is right.

Be careful to obey all these words that I command you, that it may go well with you and with your children after you forever, when you do what is good and right in the sight of the LORD your God. (Deut. 12:28)

Even to old age and gray hairs,
  O God, do not forsake me,
until I proclaim your might to another generation,
  your power to all those to come. (Ps. 71:18)

The steadfast love of the LORD is from everlasting to
    everlasting on those who fear him,
  and his righteousness to children's children. (Ps. 103:17)

I am reminded of your sincere faith, a faith that dwelt first in your grandmother Lois and your mother Eunice and now, I am sure, dwells in you as well. (2 Tim. 1:5)

3. As with our children, it may be appropriate to share with our grandchildren not only our successes but also some of our failures.

4. When possible, and after prayerful consideration, we may be led to leave our grandchildren a monetary inheritance. "A good man leaves an inheritance to his children's children" (Prov. 13:22). Admittedly, our grandchildren could use this to their harm, but it may open doors of service to good that would otherwise be closed. I know of some young people who are able to serve God full time because their grandparents helped them pay off student loans.

5. While the Bible speaks of the many positive contributions a grandparent can make to a grandchild, it also issues warnings and examples of how the life of a grandparent can have harmful effects not only on this generation of children and grandchildren but for generations to come. The Lord visits "the iniquity of the fathers on the children and the children's children, to the third and the fourth generation" (Ex. 34:7).

Grandparent Roles

Grandparents can play several roles in the lives of their grandchildren.

Best friends. These are the grandparents who get down on the child's level, playing with them and affirming their value. They provide the hugs, the laps to sit on, and unqualified acceptance. They will plan activities to enjoy together and create good memories.

Supporters. These are the grandparents who join the parents in seeking to discern the child's natural abilities, and to support and encourage them. They'll buy their grandchildren the right toys, pay for private lessons, send them to special summer camps, and generally help them find their direction in life.

Disciple-makers. In partnership with the parents, these grandparents will intentionally spend time with the grandchildren to teach, encourage, and model their faith and walk with God.

They'll plan regular times with the children and set an agenda for what's to be accomplished each time.

For younger children, this will involve reading Bible stories from an age-appropriate book, memorizing Scripture together, and (as they grow older) talking about problems the child is facing. Dorothy loves to sing the spiritual songs and choruses with our grandchildren that we sang when we were their age.

As children get older, it's helpful to simply read the Scriptures with them, commenting on the text as you go. We were taught an important lesson when our boys were young: never underestimate the ability of a child. They may be capable of understanding much more than we give them credit for. A wise piece of advice we once were given is that our children could be the greatest disciples we would ever have. Now we see that in the context of our grandchildren.

A further critical role for grandparents is to be diligent in prayer for their family. Our practice is to pray for each of our immediate family by name in our twice-a-day times of prayer—when we waken and just before we go to sleep. I remember Dorothy commenting after our parents were gone how much she missed the confidence that they were daily praying for us.

As a retired couple, we need to pray that God will give us a vision for how he would use us in the life of our family. We want to ensure that we leave our family a legacy of godliness. This may include lessons we teach, but likely more important is being an example they can imitate. A passion for God and godliness, humility, honesty, faithfulness, joy, kindness, love, serving, and hard work—these are all things our grandchildren can learn by our example.

Unfortunately for a variety of reasons some children you know may not have grandparents in their lives. Especially if you have no grandchildren of your own either as a couple or a single, talk to their parents and ask if you could begin to do things with these kids and become their "grandma" or "grandpa." The eternal rewards may be rich for them as well as for you.

Involvement with family may be the greatest way we can glorify God in retirement.

Questions to Ponder

1. List some of the strengths and weaknesses of your marriage.

2. If you are not married, is there another single with whom you can build a deep mutually supportive friendship implementing some of the principles in this strategy?

3. In retirement, would you be wiser to take on service projects together with your spouse, or separately?

4. In what ways do your children (or other younger adults) look to you for help and guidance?

5. What role are you called to play in the lives of your grandchildren?

6. In light of what we've discussed for this strategy of enjoying and strengthening your family, what changes are you committed to make in your life?

PRAYER

Gracious Father, I count my spouse, family, and other especially close friends as some of your greatest blessings. Thank you for each of them. Short of my knowledge of you, there's nothing I treasure more. I look to you to guide me in ways that will allow these relationships to glorify you more.

I need your wisdom to know what my relationships with my children and grandchildren should look like in my retirement, and what steps I should take to develop these. I desire to be part of the way you will glorify yourself in my family and close friends. Amen.

Avoid Destructive Pitfalls

I'M SURE ALL OF US have seen poor choices derail a good re-tirement. Therefore, one of our essential priorities is to develop strategies to avoid those destructive choices. None of these are typically obvious to the person affected at the outset. They all start slowly, and though apparent sometimes to others, they aren't recognized by the person involved till the situation is out of control.

Most of us have a degree of pride and self-confidence that tells us these pitfalls may happen to someone else, but not to us. Unfortunately, they could happen to any of us, and we need to have the humility to acknowledge that.

The best strategy is to recognize these pitfalls early and get help before our lives are torn up by them.

Sin

Many of us get to retirement with a host of ungodly attitudes and behaviors. Retirement is a good time to examine our lives, and with the help of the Holy Spirit we can begin to weed out these negative traits.

Perhaps we've let the world transform our character into its own mold of pride, selfish desires, and sinful thoughts. The apostle John warns us about that: "For all that is in the world—the desires of the flesh and the desires of the eyes and pride of life—is not from the Father but is from the world" (1 John 2:16). Let's face it. Our years of experience and maturity do not protect us from sin. Even in our later years, we'll continue to battle against it. The experience of Paul can be that of the retiree as well:

> I find it to be a law that when I want to do right, evil lies close at hand. For I delight in the law of God, in my inner being, but I see in my members another law waging war against the law of my mind and making me captive to the law of sin that dwells in my members. (Rom. 7:21–23)

I remember a well-known seminary professor recalling his pastor-father's prayer: "God, keep me from the sins of old men." Shortly after hearing that, I met with a group of seniors and asked them directly, "What are the sins of old men and old women?" Their list was instructive. It included self-pity, pride, stubbornness, self-centeredness, worry, unholy discontent, inappropriate anger, lack of trust, and sexual preoccupations. That's an extensive list, and frankly it's not too different from a list that younger people would come up with.

If you analyze the list, it's not too hard to see that most of these sins involve excess attention to self. Preoccupation with any one of these sins can be destructive, and must be recognized, confessed to God (and possibly to others), and then assiduously avoided with the help of the indwelling Holy Spirit.

Sexual sin, more commonly in fantasy but sometimes in practice, is common during the retirement years. It may occur more often than we recognize that an older man leaves the wife of his youth emotionally, and builds a real or imagined alliance with another woman he finds more attractive. Older women can begin to fantasize what it would be like to be married to another man. Even if only in their imagination, they become increasingly unhappy and dissatisfied with their spouse. And pornography in any of its many forms is another sexual pitfall that can become a debilitating sin for seniors.

We won't conquer sin by ourselves. It must be a work of God within us. Our strategy to deal with sin must be like that of David:

> Search me, O God, and know my heart!
>> Try me and know my thoughts!
> And see if there be any grievous way in me. (Ps. 139:23–24)

> Have mercy on me, O God,
>> according to your steadfast love;
> according to your abundant mercy
>> blot out my transgressions.
> Wash me thoroughly from my iniquity,
>> and cleanse me from my sin! (Ps. 51:1–2)

> Create in me a clean heart, O God,
>> and renew a right spirit within me. (Ps. 51:10)

Once God shows you your "grievous way," cry out for his mercy. Then ask him to keep you from future sin. It may then be helpful to seek pastoral help, or to make yourself accountable to a mature Christian friend.

Selfish Independence

Believe it or not, as helpful as an independent spirit can be in the strong and healthy years of retirement, it can become destructive in the older years as physical abilities and cognition decline. Being overly independent can lead to our being so stubborn that others find it difficult to want to help and provide care for us.

For some, independence is nothing more than an expression of sinful pride. I've often spoken to my patients about the ministry of dependence—how we help others by not being so fiercely independent. I think of Frank, who insisted on living by himself in his own home. He was so fixed on this that he failed to recognize the huge sacrifices his son was making to maintain the house, or that his daughter-in-law was making to prepare Frank's meals and ensure that the refrigerator was filled with fresh good food. If Frank had taken time to consider the full cost of his independence, he could have made wiser choices.

I've frequently seen a tension between seniors who make independence their priority, and their children who emphasize safety. Sally came to my office with her parents, who were in their nineties, insisting I tell them to sell their house, because her father had fallen changing a light bulb and she was afraid bigger problems would come. Sally's concern was legitimate, but her folks humbly spoke of their desire to be independent, and that their finances were limited and they did not want to be a burden. I tried to explain that this wasn't an issue of where they should live but a conflict of basic values: independence versus safety. They needed to discuss it on that level. Though I didn't raise it in our discussion, I felt that part of Sally's concern was somewhat selfish—she didn't want to be bothered when her parents needed help.

It's often the people we're closest to—the ones who help us most—who recognize when our selfish independence is becoming a problem. Unfortunately, they're often slow to bring it up, not wanting to appear as complaining. Here a frank talk is necessary.

Those being harmed by this spirit of independence should initiate the discussion before they're totally burned out.

Worry and Anxiety

Too many seniors are worriers. They often worry about finances, about their health, or about their spouse's health. Their worry usually centers on specific matters over which they have no control.

Worry can cause physical problems such as insomnia, headaches, high blood pressure, abdominal pain, or any number of other conditions. Perhaps more important, worry can be a spiritual problem.

All too often, worry is associated with too high a view of ourselves, thinking we deserve to have everything go well. This may amount to nothing more than pride. Or worry can represent too low a view of God. If we really believe God is loving, powerful, and in control, we should be able to trust him without fear. The writer of Hebrews alludes to Psalm 118 when he reminds us, "We can confidently say, 'The Lord is my helper; / I will not fear; / what can man do to me?'" (Heb. 13:6).

Paul provides helpful strategies for handling worry:

The Lord is at hand; do not be anxious about anything, but in everything by prayer and supplication with thanksgiving let your requests be made known to God. And the peace of God, which surpasses all understanding, will guard your hearts and your minds in Christ Jesus. Finally, brothers, whatever is true, whatever is honorable, whatever is just, whatever is pure, whatever is lovely, whatever is commendable, if there is any excellence, if there is anything worthy of praise, think about these things. What you have learned and received and heard and seen in me—practice these things, and the God of peace will be with you. (Phil. 4:5–9)

Note the following points from Paul's teaching:

- The phrase "The Lord is at hand" emphasizes that Jesus is not only near us today but will soon return for us. That should give us a true perspective on our current problems.
- We should be praying to God for his intervention in the problems we face. He may choose to resolve the situation, or he may give us peace and the ability to endure.
- Rather than focusing on the immediate problem, we should be thankful for the many ways God has helped us in the past, and be grateful for the hope that he'll help with our present need.
- In coming openly before him with our needs, we should expect to experience God's peace, even though we may not understand how our situation has changed.
- Once we feel that peace, we should expect him to guard our hearts and minds to keep us from falling back into the pattern of worry.
- We need to move on from what we were worried about and focus our minds on things that are good.

Depression

Mild depressive feelings are commonly associated with adjusting to retirement, as we addressed in strategy 3. But a more severely disabling form of depression is all too common in later years.

Picture the stereotypical grumpy old person who won't take the initiative to get up and do something, but is always complaining, apathetic, and lazy. Though this may be just "how they are," these symptoms may also be signs of severe depression. Admittedly, some people are genetically predisposed to depression, and others have been the innocent victims of a distressing life event (resulting in post-traumatic stress disorder). But for some, depression is the consequence of their cumulative life's experiences.

Other causes of depression include isolation, strained relationships, recurrent failures, chronic pain, and side effects of some hypertension medications. For some, there may be spiritual issues leading to depression.

It's common for depression itself to lead to poor choices that make a person irritable, which in turn can make the depression worse, creating a vicious cycle. Depression can also lead to laziness and a lack of the motivation to seek help. Another common theme of retirees is hypochondriasis—constantly talking and thinking about their ailments. This is another expression of worry and depression.

The good news is that depression in many of its forms may be treatable. If possible, it's best to get to the root of the problem. In addition, antidepressant medications are typically safe and effective. These can usually be prescribed by a primary care professional or by a psychiatrist.

Some Christians experience spiritual depression.[1] They might lack a deep assurance of God's saving grace. For others, depression may be rooted in false expectations of God and our resulting disappointment with him. Many Christians lack a robust understanding of how God uses the difficulties of life to accomplish his greater purposes. When things get tough, they begin to question God's goodness and love.

1   The classic and excellent book on this is *Spiritual Depression: Its Causes and Its Cure* by D. Martyn Lloyd-Jones (Grand Rapids, MI: Eerdmans, 1965).

Whatever the root of the depression, it may help to seek pastoral counsel. This should usually be done before pursuing antidepressant medications.

Substance Abuse

Studies show that alcohol and substance abuse become a problem for 10 to 15 percent of Americans over sixty-five.[2] Alcohol is the biggest offender in substance abuse.

These problems typically begin innocently, such as enjoying a glass of wine with dinner or as part of winding down before going to bed. But if not kept within strict daily limits (one drink only, whether wine, cocktail, or beer, since they all contain similar amounts of alcohol), this can quickly escalate and become a problem. In some of my patients with early dementia, I've seen that just one glass of wine wipes out their memories; then they have another glass, thinking it was their first.

As is widely publicized, abuse of prescription drugs is common among seniors. This can include prescription painkillers, tranquilizers, or sleeping pills. All these are addicting, and the longer you take them, the less effective they are. This leads to the temptation to take a higher dose. The more painkillers you take, the more they lower your tolerance for pain. The more sleeping pills or sedatives you take, the less you're able to cope with the common stressors of life.

Poor Biblical Examples

The reality of poor choices that wreck the older years is a theme well known to the Bible. Consider the following.

2   Rakesh Lal and Raman Deep Pattanayak, "Alcohol Use among the Elderly: Issues and Considerations," *Journal of Geriatric Mental Health*, 4, no. 1 (2017), https://www.jgmh.org /article.asp?issn=2348-9995;year=2017;volume=4;issue=1;spage=4;epage=10;aulast=Lal.

Solomon—seeking ungodly pleasure. We all probably know the story of Solomon's good start in life: blessed by his father David, asking not for wealth or longevity but rather for wisdom, and building the fabulous temple in Jerusalem. Yet later in his life he gave in to temptations for illicit marriages, to enjoy sexual pleasure and manipulate international relationships. We read: "When Solomon was old his wives turned away his heart after other gods, and his heart was not wholly true to the LORD his God" (1 Kings 11:4).

Asa—not keeping faith. King Asa was another king of Judah who started well, but toward the end of his life, rather than trusting the Lord for victory over an enemy, he forged an alliance with the king of Syria. He then developed a terminal illness (apparently something like gangrene in his feet), and refused to consult the Lord. Having started strong, he later wavered in his faith.

Hezekiah—peace at any price. King Hezekiah was another man who had a brilliant start. He saw God act dramatically to defeat the Assyrians, but then his pride got the best of him, and he pridefully showed off his wealth to Assyrian emissaries in an apparent effort to keep the peace. He ended poorly.

Josiah—taking inappropriate risk. King Josiah had instituted many godly reforms for his people. In his later years, the king of Egypt was headed through Judah to confront the Babylonians. He didn't intend to fight Josiah. Nevertheless, Josiah challenged Pharaoh—whether out of arrogance, or lack of wisdom, or through some unknown misunderstanding. Josiah then was killed in this unnecessary battle.

———

Retirement can be rather fragile. It can provide a lot of good for our lives, but it doesn't take much of a mistake to destroy retirement's potential to give glory to God. Jesus warned of those who "hear, but as they go on their way they are choked by the cares and riches and pleasures of life, and their fruit does not mature" (Luke 8:14). Likewise Paul spoke of Demas, who "in love with this present world, has deserted me" (2 Tim. 4:10). And the apostle John wrote of those who "went out from us, but they were not of us; for if they had been of us, they would have continued with us. But they went out, that it might become plain that they all are not of us" (1 John 2:19).

All of this doesn't mean that those of us who have been saved by God's grace are in danger of losing our salvation—and for this I'm grateful. But when we're tempted to turn our backs on the Lord, this should challenge us to reaffirm our trust in the Lord. Our assurance that we've truly trusted Jesus will then be even stronger.

Given our weakness and tendency to err, it will only be by God's grace that we'll finish our earthly lives well. Most of us can identify with these lines from Robert Robinson's hymn "Come, Thou Fount of Every Blessing": "Prone to wander, Lord, I feel it; prone to leave the God I love."[3] But also recall the familiar and encouraging words from John Newton's "Amazing Grace": "'Tis grace hath brought me safe thus far, and grace will lead me home."[4] We need that grace to keep us from destructive behaviors.

Questions to Ponder

1. Are there any sins in your life that you know have the potential to derail your ability to glorify God in your retirement?

---

3   Robert Robinson, "Come, Thou Fount of Every Blessing," 1758, in *Trinity Hymnal* (Suwanee, GA: Great Commission Publications, 1990), no. 457.

4   John Newton, "Amazing Grace," 1779, in *Trinity Hymnal* (Suwanee, GA: Great Commission Publications,1990), no. 460.

2. Do you appreciate that your desire for independence could in time cause increased difficulties for your family?

3. Do you have a weakness for alcohol or potentially habit-forming medications?

4. Are you becoming too stubborn?

5. In light of what we've discussed for this strategy of avoiding destructive pitfalls, what changes are you committed to make in your life?

PRAYER

Heavenly Father, I know that there are times when I'm my own worst enemy. As I progress through retirement, I need you, by your Holy Spirit living in me, to protect me from making wrong and foolish choices. Keep me pure in my actions and thoughts until you call me into your holy presence.

I pray this, lest my poor decisions discredit your holy name. For the sake of Jesus. Amen.

Get Busy

FREQUENTLY MY PATIENTS would come in for a complete physical checkup before they retired. They had no doubt heard about people who dropped dead the day they retired—and they didn't want to be among them.

At the end of my exam, I would ask these patients if I could give them my two retirement rules. Of course, everyone said yes.

The rules were simple:

1. Wake up every morning knowing what you're going to do that day.

2. Go to bed every night knowing that you helped someone that day.

I would then explain that retirement isn't to be a permanent vacation. It's not a time to sit around doing nothing except thinking about yourself and your own happiness. If you do approach it that way, you'll likely be miserable—and make everyone around you miserable too.

I made the point in strategy 5 that your retirement should start with a sabbatical, when you relax, unwind, get your batteries recharged, and again enjoy time with Jesus, family, and friends. After you've done all that—however long it takes—then it's time to get busy working for the Lord. But do it in such a way that you preserve a balance among your other priorities. You'll also likely find that if you go at it with a slower pace and don't put yourself under pressure, you'll enjoy being busy again.

Keep in mind that work is good for us. It's what we were made for. Recall the point we made earlier that even before Adam sinned, God gave him a job to do—caring for the garden. Work wasn't a punishment. Work itself was never part of the curse for Adam's sin; but that curse did give our work a more onerous and difficult character.

When I commented on how busy one patient kept himself, he answered with a smile on his face: "John, I can't lie down—they'll start throwing dirt on top of me!" There's no reason to sit around and not keep active. The old motto *carpe diem*—seize the day—applies here. There's a race in progress, so get off the sidelines and join the other runners. Time may be short—the end will soon be in sight.

Recall some of the scriptures we read in the introduction about our responsibility to serve God in our later days.

Do you not know that in a race all the runners run, but only one receives the prize? So run that you may obtain it. Every athlete exercises self-control in all things. They do it to receive a perishable wreath, but we an imperishable. So I do not run aimlessly; I do not box as one beating the air. But I discipline my body and keep it under control, lest after preaching to others I myself should be disqualified. (1 Cor. 9:24–27)

The image of the race is memorably presented also in this passage:

> Since we are surrounded by so great a cloud of witnesses, let
> us also lay aside every weight, and sin which clings so closely,
> and let us run with endurance the race that is set before us,
> looking to Jesus, the founder and perfecter of our faith, who
> for the joy that was set before him endured the cross, despis-
> ing the shame, and is seated at the right hand of the throne of
> God. (Heb. 12:1–2)

Picture yourself running on the track in front of a stadium
filled with saints who have gone before, all of them cheering you
on. Can you see Job? And Moses? How about Elijah, David, and
myriads of others? Listen, and you may hear: "Keep going! Press
on, give it your all! Finish hard!" See the finish line, and know
that Jesus is there with a smile on his face and arms stretched out,
waiting to welcome you to your eternal rest.

This is no time for slacking, so press on for as many years as
God allows. You've had your sabbatical, you know your priorities
and what you want to accomplish, and your eternal rest is yet
to come. Now—while life remains—get busy and run well till
your race is won.

George Sweeting, former president of Moody Bible Institute,
wrote the following words with his son, Pastor Don Sweeting,
then president of Colorado Christian University:

> As long as you have today, make it count. Don't wait for some
> future day to start living for Christ. Do so now. You belong to
> Him. So, given all that He has done for you, give yourself now
> wholeheartedly to Him. Find the joy that is found in Christ
> today! Use what you have left for Christ and His kingdom.

Persevere. Go the distance. By the power of the Holy Spirit, commit yourself today to live the rest of your days without regret.[1]

Let your goal be to reach the end of your life in the same manner Paul did:

> I have fought the good fight, I have finished the race, I have kept the faith. Henceforth there is laid up for me the crown of righteousness, which the Lord, the righteous judge, will award to me on that day, and not only to me but also to all who have loved his appearing. (2 Tim. 4:7–8)

> So we do not lose heart. Though our outer self is wasting away, our inner self is being renewed day by day. For this light momentary affliction is preparing for us an eternal weight of glory beyond all comparison, as we look not to the things that are seen but to the things that are unseen. For the things that are seen are transient, but the things that are unseen are eternal. (2 Cor. 4:16–18)

Someday we will meet our Lord and Savior face to face. We'll be accountable to him for the way we have spent our retirement years. Let us keep busy and look forward to his smile as he says, "Well done, good and faithful servant. . . . Enter into the joy of your master" (Matt. 25:21).

Now, as much as always, we must not forget that we're to offer our bodies as a "living sacrifice, holy and acceptable to God, which is your spiritual worship" (Rom. 12:1).

1   Donald W. Sweeting and George Sweeting, *How to Finish the Christian Life: Following Jesus in the Second Half* (Chicago: Moody, 2012), 196.

Do Good

Whatever activity God will lead us into, it must allow us to do good for others and to help them.

Doing good is a strong theme throughout the Scriptures. Those "who have believed in God" are told to "be careful to devote themselves to good works. These things are excellent and profitable for people" (Titus 3:8). As you consider the following additional verses, the necessity for spending our lives doing good will be loud and clear:

Jesus . . . went about doing good. (Acts 10:38)

For we are his workmanship, created in Christ Jesus for good works, which God prepared beforehand, that we should walk in them. (Eph. 2:10)

Do good . . . be rich in good works . . . be generous and ready to share. (1 Tim. 6:18)

Be ready for every good work. (Titus 3:1)

The saying is trustworthy, and I want you to insist on these things, so that those who have believed in God may be careful to devote themselves to good works. These things are excellent and profitable for people (Titus 3:8).

Let our people learn to devote themselves to good works, so as to help cases of urgent need, and not be unfruitful. (Titus 3:14)

Learn to do good;
    seek justice,

correct oppression;
   bring justice to the fatherless,
plead the widow's cause. (Isa. 1:17)

Do not neglect to do good and to share what you have, for such sacrifices are pleasing to God. (Heb. 13:16).

Jesus Christ . . . gave himself for us to redeem us from all lawlessness and to purify for himself a people for his own possession who are zealous for good works. (Titus 2:13–14)

Think about how closely goodness is associated with God's glory. It's instructive that in Exodus 33, when Moses asked to see God's glory, God responded, "I will make all my goodness pass before you" (Ex. 33:19). When we think of the glory of God, many of his attributes may come to mind, but apparently God equates his glory with his goodness.

In much the same way, Jesus links God's glory with our good works: "Let your light shine before others, so that they may see your good works and give glory to your Father who is in heaven" (Matt. 5:16). Peter echoes this when he instructs us to live so that others "may see your good deeds and glorify God" (1 Pet. 2:12).

With such a weight of Scripture on this topic, it's no wonder that John Wesley would say:

Do all the good you can,
by all the means you can,
in all the ways you can,
in all the places you can,
at all the times you can,

to all the people you can,

as long as ever you can.[2]

Do Things with Eternal Impact

Another important consideration is that whatever we do will have results that last into eternity. Missionary C. T. Studd (1860–1931) composed a poem repeating this phrase: "Only one life, 'twill soon be past, only what's done for Christ will last." Jesus instructed his disciples, "Do not work for the food that perishes, but for the food that endures to eternal life" (John 6:27).

When counseling Christian medical students, I frequently discuss the question of their future specialty. The school's faculty rightly advises them to consider their abilities and their passions when making that choice. These things are certainly critical. But in my discussions with them, I always add a third consideration. I ask them in what field they could have more eternal impact to glorify God by doing good for others.

These same questions about abilities, passions, and glorifying God are essential when considering what to do in retirement.

We should be aware that these factors—doing good and glorifying God—may limit how much time we spend on our own entertainment and recreation. But hopefully, our doing good with eternal benefit will bring us great joy and satisfaction. We should also be mindful that if we aren't careful and we go overboard in doing good in our retirement, our lives might become just as much out of balance as our working life was. We must still have time for other priorities. If not, we could burn out—or as Paul says, become "weary in doing good" (2 Thess. 3:13).

2   From John Wesley's "Directions to Penitents and Believers, for Renewing Their Covenant with God," as quoted in *Dangerous Prayers: 50 Powerful Prayers That Changed the World*, compiled by Susan Hill (Nashville: Thomas Nelson, 2019), 188.

Spend Time with Younger People

Scripture makes it clear that one way we're to spend time in retirement is with younger people.

> Older men are to be sober-minded, dignified, self-controlled,
> sound in faith, in love, and in steadfastness. Older women
> likewise are to be reverent in behavior, not slanderers or slaves
> to much wine. They are to teach what is good, and so train
> the young women to love their husbands and children, to be
> self-controlled, pure, working at home, kind, and submissive to
> their own husbands, that the word of God may not be reviled.
> (Titus 2:2–5)

Older men and women need to accept their role as seniors, and
to embrace the fact that they have something to offer those who
are younger. There's no reason to be embarrassed by being older.
Job had it right when he said, "Wisdom is with the aged, and
understanding in length of days" (Job 12:12). In my seventies, I
don't have as much knowledge as I would like, but by God's grace
I may have some wisdom.

True, you're getting older, and you may feel that your "outer
self is wasting away" (2 Cor. 4:16), but that doesn't necessarily
mean you're lacking spiritual vigor, or that you can't continue
playing a significant role in the lives of others.

The characteristics listed in that Titus passage particularly for
older men—sobriety, dignity, self-control, and soundness in faith,
love, and steadfastness—should serve as a model for all stages of
life. These can be passed on only by spending time with younger
men. Similarly, older women are to be models of reverent behav-
ior, being careful not to slander others in their speech, avoiding the

excessive use of alcohol, and—more prominently—being actively involved in teaching younger women. How that is done will vary from person to person. The point is that it *should* be done.

At times we must go out of our way to ensure this intergenerational friendship. It's not always the default, particularly in church settings—where it's particularly important. Churches with active programs for seniors must ensure that there are opportunities for fellowship and friendship that cross generational lines. Otherwise, seniors tend to spend all their time with each other. My experience has been that the younger generation is openly looking for this wisdom.

Seek God's Will

The question of how we spend whatever time remains after our other priorities are met requires us to seek God's will. We often find no specific guidance in Scripture about what to do in our specific circumstance, so the answer will vary from person to person.

Understanding God's will starts with five basic premises.

1. God's will isn't some mystical secret which we either follow to receive his blessing or become disqualified through our failure to find it, with our lives forfeit. God's will is never taught that way in Scripture. More likely, his will is simply wisdom. He is the source of all wisdom (Job 12:13), and if we want his wisdom to direct us, we must start with a deep respect for the Lord (Prov. 9:10), while having complete trust in him rather than in our own understanding (Prov. 3:5–6). Thankfully, the Lord is willing to give us his wisdom when we pray for it (Prov. 2:6; James 1:5).

2. God has given us a great deal of clear and specific direction in Scripture. We've already seen how we must do good for others, do things that will have eternal impact, and spend time with younger people. We need not ask if such things are his will.

3. Few decisions in life are irreversible. If we feel that God is leading us in a particular direction, and it later proves to be a fiasco, there's no harm with stopping, redirecting, and setting off in a new direction. The GPS on my phone is very gentle with me. It knows where I am, and if I tell it where I want to go, it tells me the best way to get there. If I don't follow instructions it gives, it doesn't yell and scream at me. It recalculates and tells me the way to go from there. Likewise, if we make a wrong decision in life, it may have been God's intention to use our "mistake" for our benefit. There's encouragement in knowing that though we make mistakes, God does not.

4. Don't limit God. Never say, "I can't do that," when he's directing you in a specific way. When our boys were small, we would read them a delightful story about a canning factory that canned "can'ts"—it took can'ts and put them into cans. We need to respond to things that seem impossible by saying, "If God truly wants me to do this, I will trust him to help, and I'll go for it." Recognize that God may lead you to accomplish surprisingly big things in your retirement. Remember that Moses took on his life's work at age eighty, when the average life expectancy was closer to thirty-five. Caleb was eighty-five when he took on a whole new project (Josh. 14:10–12). Missionary pioneer William Carey is famous for saying, "Expect great things; attempt great things."[3]

5. Sometimes we discern God's will by trial and error. That's okay. It may be appropriate to make minimal initial commitments. You might commit to serving with a ministry to the needy in your community three mornings a week for the next three months, and afterward reconsider and evaluate how it's going. There's no point in pursuing something with a stubborn arrogance

---

3   William Carey (sermon, Friar Lane Baptist Chapel, Nottingham, England, May 30, 1792).

to never quit or readjust. We'll see in our next strategy that our abilities will change over the years of our retirement, and we'll need to be flexible. What's wise for us to do early in retirement may not be so wise down the line.

Now that we understand these basics, we come back to the question of how to practically go about choosing the way we spend our spare time in retirement. We'll consider a general strategy, and then get down to specifics.

Start by making a regular commitment to pray for God's wisdom and direction. Ask the Holy Spirit to bring thoughts to your mind and to control circumstances that may help set your course. If you're married, pray together with your spouse for guidance and wisdom as to whether you're best to work together or separately. If together, pray for unity about what to do. Along with praying, spend time in the Scriptures, asking God by his Spirit to show you principles that can help you decide.

In addition to the wisdom we get from Scripture and the leading of the Holy Spirit, look to others for wise counsel. Dorothy and I started to carefully plan a strategy for how to decide what to do in retirement several years before we were to fully retire. We listened to a series of talks about God's guidance, and then sat down with one of our pastors and his wife to get their ideas. We spoke to our children, to close friends, and to leaders of several local service organizations. We're now sorting through several options.

What to Do with Discretionary Time

When I talk to people planning to retire, one of their first responses is usually, "What am I going to do all day?"[4]

---

4 This is a common enough question for retirees, as evidenced in the title of a book by Patrice Jenkins: *What Will I Do All Day? Wisdom to Get You Over Retirement and On with Living!* (Engelsen, 2011).

As you've seen, I've deliberately avoided that question till now. I've done this because I feel strongly that whatever specific task we take up in our retirement is less important than the other strategies we've reviewed. Doing justice to our other priorities comes first and will take a lot of our time, but it isn't likely to keep us busy *all* the time. If you're like me, you don't want to waste time or be bored. You need a plan for how to spend the time left over.

If you can afford to go without a salary, don't plan to get a full-time job. That will be too much, and soon your life will be out of balance again. But chances are excellent that you'll be able to maintain the balanced life you seek and still have time to commit to some type of part-time work on a regular basis. Hopefully, it will involve doing good, have an eternal impact, and keep you in touch with younger people and with people who need Jesus.

Let me share some of the things to consider as you approach the what-should-I-do question.

1. As with those medical students, ask yourself: What are my passions? What skills do I have to offer? Is there something I've been just itching to get into, but haven't been able to—something that would bring glory to God by meeting the three criteria of doing good, having eternal impact, and influencing younger friends?

Perhaps it's a hobby club, something you've wanted to study and learn, singing in a chorus, playing in a music group, teaching a class—the list of possibilities is endless. It may be that God has placed that kind of desire in you, and it's unwise to ignore it.

How has God uniquely equipped you to serve your church? Think about your spiritual gifts. In what ways do you derive great pleasure as you serve others?

2. It may be wise to ask what you enjoy most about your current job. What are you good at doing? What gives you meaning and

purpose? Also think about what you enjoy least. From there, ask God to show you some ways to continue doing what you enjoy most and to avoid what you enjoy least.

For myself, I really enjoy talking to people about their problems and advising them in ways that may help them. What I don't enjoy is documenting that visit in the computer. Is it possible I'll find a way to enjoy the good without the bad?

As you look back over your working years, can you see how God may have been preparing you for your next step?

3. Ask also how much structure you want or need in your life. If you choose not to make regular commitments, will opportunities to serve arise with sufficient regularity that you'll be using your time efficiently? Will you be happily busy, or bored? How much structure do you need to keep from wasting your God-given time waiting for opportunities to serve?

Early in retirement, without any commitments, you may enjoy the freedom to spontaneously choose what to do each day. This may work well during your sabbatical. Before long, though, you may find that it's more work *not* to work. It's hard to have to look each day for ways to serve. When you start to feel that way, it's likely time to have more structure in your life. An example would be to commit to three mornings a week to helping at the local library. Having made that commitment, then you get up and go, whether you feel like it or not. Frankly, my observation has been that most people are happier with a regular schedule.

4. Volunteering is a great option to provide some structure for those who don't need more income. Volunteering allows you to choose what you do based on the potential for doing good and having an eternal impact, with a motivation that goes beyond making money.

Your voluntary service can be either formal or informal. Formal volunteering usually involves a firm commitment to spend a certain number of hours each week in serving, with agreed upon times off. It means learning a job and working with a supervisor who will depend on you to do what you've agreed to do. My brother-in-law Jim has volunteered at his local hospital for years. He typically sits at the outpatient surgery registration desk, welcomes people, and helps them feel comfortable while they wait. He loves it, and I know the patients appreciate him. A cousin volunteers with his wife in the home office of the mission agency that their daughter and son-in-law serve with. It provides them with meaningful, eternally significant activity, allows them to work together, and keeps them busy.

The options of where to volunteer with a formal commitment will vary with your community, but will often include church or community organizations such as homeless shelters, hospitals, libraries, schools, and park districts.

Informal volunteering is another option. It doesn't involve a commitment or provide much structure, and though it gives more freedom, it may not keep you sufficiently busy. Our churches and communities offer many options for informal volunteering. It seems there are always calls to fill openings on ad hoc committees looking for seniors to serve. We hear of people who need meals, rides, or household chores done. The advantage of informal volunteering is that it allows you to step in and serve when it fits your schedule, and doesn't interfere with your other priorities.

Many larger churches have paid staff providing leadership and services to their senior members. These pastors for seniors will organize programs and social events, teach classes, and serve the pastoral needs of seniors in the church. Smaller churches need volunteers to fill those roles.

5. Identify the obvious immediate needs around you. How about your neighbors, church, community, or city? What are the apparent needs?

Jeff Haanen encourages us to ask what God is doing in the world that you feel passionate about.[5] Some examples he gives include:

- Environment and climate change
- Justice and racial disparity
- Ethical issues such as abortion, assisted suicide, or transgenderism
- Politics, whether local, statewide, or national
- Homelessness
- Poverty
- Drug addiction
- Education

Most communities have groups of volunteers who are involved in these areas of need. Working with them can provide a significant means to glorify God as you build diverse friendships and focus on the needs of others. Remember Paul's exhortation to the Philippians: "Let each of you look not only to his own interests, but also to the interests of others" (Phil. 2:4). Perhaps you need to ask the Lord to give you a passion for one of these areas where you could serve.

6. Are you looking forward to new challenges or acquiring a new skill? That may depend on how you're doing mentally. If you're able and eager to take on a new challenge, go for it. You may find it enjoyable and energizing. If you feel that you're not quite as sharp or energetic as you once were, you may be frustrated

---

5 Jeff Haanen, *An Uncommon Guide to Retirement: Finding God's Purpose for the Next Season of Life*, (Chicago: Moody, 2019), 68.

doing something that requires more thinking and learning. But there are still many others ways in which you can serve.

7. Recognize that some retirees (particularly those who are younger when they retire) may be called to entirely new realms of service, or to go back to school and retrain for an entirely new career. This may lead to full-time ministry, whether in this country or in international missions.

8. If all this is confusing, and you need more practical direction, consider working with a retirement coach. These are trained professionals who can help you find a good fit in your retirement. Some of these are committed Christians.[6]

Questions to Ponder

1. After considering your other priorities, how much time do you think you'll have each week for other scheduled activities?

2. If you're married, would you and your spouse envision doing things together?

3. If you choose not to have regularly scheduled activities, can you live productively without structure, or would you tend to waste time?

4. Do any of the contemporary issues listed above grab your attention?

5. In light of what we've discussed for this strategy of keeping appropriately busy, what changes are you committed to make in your life?

---

6   See the websites for the Retirement Coaches Association (https://www.retirementcoaches association.org/) and the Christian Coaches Network International (https://christian coaches.com/).

PRAYER

Gracious Father, you continue to bless me with health and energy, and now—in retirement—you bless me also with time. I want to spend this time in ways that are consistent with your values. You've allowed me this time; now direct me to use it wisely and efficiently as a good steward for your glory. Please help me to use my discretionary time to bring you glory in the most effective ways. Show me if I should pursue a paid job, and if so, what that should be. Or if it's best that I volunteer, how should I go about it? Lead me to wise counselors who can guide me.

Help me to be faithfully praying for your direction. I offer these years to you as a living sacrifice. I pray this for your glory and my good. Amen.

Be Flexible, Adaptable, and Resilient

CONSTANT CHANGE IS ONE of the stark realities of retirement—and the older we are, the faster change comes. This shouldn't surprise us, for by the time we reach retirement age, we've already been through a lot of change. Some has been the result of choices we've made, and some was not of our choosing. We can be confident, however, that all the changes we've experienced in the past—and all those we'll experience in the future—are the result of God's good providence.

Strategy 6 spoke of pitfalls we need to avoid to keep from derailing a good retirement. Most of these pitfalls result from our own poor choices. Now we'll talk about changes that we cannot control. For these, we must trust that God is in control, trust him to do what's best, adjust to the permanent changes, and develop a resilience to bounce back from any short-term setbacks.

Stages in Retirement

Though each person's retirement will be different, several researchers have identified a rather stereotypical pattern that many of our retirements will go through.[1] Here's my own list of these stages:

1. *Catching up.* Right after we retire, we're naturally busy. Our to-do list has been growing for years, and now we have freedom to focus on things we've been putting off. Necessary chores may include reviewing finances (including estate plans), getting on Medicare or other health insurance, doing neglected home and car repairs or maintenance, having a physical, and getting into an exercise program. More enjoyable activities may include travel and spending more time with family and friends who live some distance away. This early stage of retirement can also be the appropriate time to fulfill some of the fun things on our bucket list, while we have the time and energy to do so.

2. *Sabbatical.* Once we've caught up with important and urgent items needing our attention, we'll want to slow down, breathe easy, and take the sabbatical we spoke of in strategy 5. It's during this time that we should carefully and prayerfully invigorate our walk with the Lord, define our priorities, and get our lives in balance. This is when we should investigate what we're going to do once we're ready to get back to regular activities.

3. *Disenchantment.* This may come after we've caught up and done our planning and prioritizing. We may start feeling somewhat restless and bored. This is the time to declare our sabbatical over, and to get back to being more productive. With God's help, we'll find new and meaningful activities—but this time we'll pursue life at a realistic pace, while keeping all our priorities in balance.

---

1 My list draws from an outline by gerontologist Robert C. Atchley, which is summarized at the *Quizlet* website, https://quizlet.com/209622109/psychology-robert-atchley-7-stages-of -retirement-flash-cards/.

4. *Stability.* We enter the new normal. We're happy, productive, and content with life's balance, and we continue to enjoy the years to come.

5. *Decline.* Most of us will experience a period of decline between our productive years and our death. Medical science has made huge advances in recent decades to shorten that decline, but unless we die suddenly, it's a stage most of us will go through. This is where we'll need to be flexible.

Prepare for the Challenges Ahead

I write this during a repeated surge of the COVID-19 virus. Despite the tragic results of this pandemic, one thing it has taught us is to be more flexible when the unexpected comes, recognizing that although such things may be a surprise to us, they never surprise God. He remains sovereign and in control, still accomplishing his purpose.

While not everything God brings into our lives can be anticipated, many things can be—and that allows us time to prepare. We're therefore wise to prayerfully consider how we will respond if God, in his loving providence, allows us to encounter some of the following hurdles.

Declining Energy and Strength

In my geriatric practice, I've seen physical declines in patients again and again. After retirement, we may continue strong and energetic for some time, but eventually our abilities begin to wane. Our retirement may start joyful and meet the expectations we had, but the road ahead may not be all that smooth, and life becomes more challenging. Some of the physical changes we experience are the natural and gradual results of aging, as we begin to lose strength and energy. This may be hard to accept, but we must respond to these gradual changes in a way consistent with our ultimate goal of bringing glory to God.

We must remind ourselves that we're running a race, and we want to finish well. The most difficult part of a race is not the start but the approach to the finish line. Several decades ago I ran my first marathon. I was at the office the next day seeing an older man I knew well. He said, "Congratulations. I heard you ran the marathon yesterday—that's twenty-six miles, isn't it?"

"No sir," I replied, quickly pointing out that it's actually 26.2 miles. "Don't forget the point-two—it's the longest two-tenths of a mile you could ever run."

As we approach the end of life's race while facing gradual decline, we should buckle down and stubbornly press on for as long as it's possible.

But there will come a time when, even with God's help, we'll have to slow down and accept change. It may be that the Sunday school class we've been teaching no longer needs us, or the grandkids we've invested in so heavily leave for college or marry and move far away. This slowing down will force us to rebalance our priorities. But our lives can still bring glory to God. We'll probably spend less time in service and more time enjoying the Lord. We'll be more like Mary and less like Martha.

A good example is a dear patient of mine who was confined to a chair, unable to get up and walk. She was still able to listen to hymns and the Scriptures on her CD player. So she would sit with a pleasant smile on her face, humming the hymns while being transformed by the presence of her Lord.

Debilitating Illness

Illness may cause temporary disability—for example, getting influenza and finding your strength zapped for several months.

Though this often happens with seniors, eventually they see full recovery. Or it may be a one-time event with incomplete recovery, as can happen with a stroke. Congestive heart failure, chronic lung disease, and kidney disease can bring frequent exacerbations that require hospitalization and rehab stays. Another progressive disability is arthritis, which can progress slowly. Unless some medical treatment intervenes, it may leave you unable to get around.

Unless there's full recovery, each exacerbation of these medical conditions will leave you a little weaker, necessitating change and rebalancing your priorities.

Some will succumb to cancer. If the disease for them is treatable, they may have to endure surgery or chemotherapy, with periods of disability that may temporarily or even permanently derail their retirement plans. For some, the cancer will prove to be terminal—and then it's time to emphasize closeness to the Lord, for they'll soon enter his presence. When faced with any terminal illness, the way to glorify God will be to live faithfully till he takes you home.

Cognitive Decline

All of us will show some age-related changes in our brains. The good news is that while brain imaging, such as an MRI, will show shrinkage called atrophy, this isn't necessarily a loss of nerve cells, and does not by itself indicate dementia. Also, there will be some inevitable changes in brain function, specifically loss of short-term memory and language. Forgetting names and words, particularly nouns, is common, and this will likewise not necessarily lead to dementia. We may no longer keep track of several things at once, and we can't multitask like we did earlier. We can be encouraged in knowing that a normal older brain, while not perfect, can still learn new things and allow for an enjoyable life.

The bad news is that roughly a third of us will die with some form of progressive dementia, the most common being Alzheimer's disease. Though there are some treatments that may slow the progression of certain kinds of dementia, there's nothing currently available to significantly halt the disease.[2] It's critically important that those with early dementia—and their caregivers—learn to recognize that God still loves and values them.

Keep in mind that our value is found not in our intelligence or ability to accomplish things, but in the fact that we're made in the image of God and loved by Jesus. People in any stage of dementia are still whole people, even though sick. They have an inherent dignity that must be respected. When others respect their dignity, it goes a long way toward improving their quality of life. A mental illness no more detracts from dignity than does a physical illness.

Pain and Suffering

Some of us will be called to endure pain and suffering during our retirement to a degree that will challenge our faith in a loving and powerful God.

We may, for example, experience the daily pain of arthritis or the excruciating pain of metastatic cancer. If this is your situation, remember that God is still in control.

I find comfort in this passage from the Psalms: "Once God has spoken; / twice have I heard this: / that power belongs to God, / and that to you, O Lord, belongs steadfast love" (Ps. 62:11–12). No matter how much pain you're experiencing, you can still affirm God's love and power—that he cares and is able to help. If you truly believe those two things in the face of great suffering, then

2   See my book *Finding Grace in the Face of Dementia* (Wheaton, IL: Crossway, 2017).

there's only one explanation for it: God has some purpose that you don't understand. David affirms that as well: "I cry out to God Most High, / to God who fulfills his purpose for me" (Ps. 57:2).

When we hurt so badly that we cry out to God for relief, we can trust that he has his purposes, and that he'll accomplish them. In this we can find assurance and hope. Meanwhile, we can be grateful that God has enabled modern medicine to do so much to help ameliorate pain and suffering.

Caregiving

Unexpectedly needing to care for a disabled spouse or another family member may necessitate drastic changes in our retirement plans. If so, it will help to recognize these things:

- First, caregiving is God's sovereign plan for you at this time in your life. It's what he has called you to.
- Second, the love you show to another person fulfills your ultimate priority and brings glory to God—even when that hasn't been your own plan.
- Third, God will be with you to strengthen you in giving care to another.
- Fourth, there's often help available to you in this, whether from family, friends, church, or community. God has provided this help, but it may require a degree of humility for you to ask for it, or even to accept it.
- Fifth, in the midst of caregiving, you may be tempted to despair, but remember God's faithfulness and grace: "No temptation has overtaken you that is not common to man. God is faithful, and he will not let you be tempted beyond your ability, but with the temptation he will also provide the way of escape, that you may be able to endure it" (1 Cor. 10:13).

The need for care often results from a slowly progressive disease like dementia. Fortunately in those situations, you can recognize that the need is coming. You can learn as much as possible about the disease and about what community resources are available, then make necessary physical changes in the house before the need is urgent.

At other times, caregiving is precipitated by an acute illness, such as a stroke or broken hip. In those cases, some time may be available to prepare while your loved one is receiving inpatient rehab. While the patient is in the hospital, social workers will be available to help direct you in getting the equipment and help you'll need.

Death of a Spouse or Other Loved Ones

The death of a spouse can be so devastating that there's little resilience to get up and get going. Some would rather lose their own lives than face life without their spouse.

When our spouse dies, we must remember the comfort from Psalm 23:

> Even though I walk through the valley of the shadow of death,
> I will fear no evil,
> for you are with me;
> your rod and your staff,
> they comfort me. (Ps. 23:4)

The valley of the shadow of death isn't necessarily our own death, but may be that of someone we love, have shared life with, and have accompanied on their final journey. We may be tempted to despair, but we can look to our Shepherd to comfort us. And with that, we can keep going through such a difficult time.

How do we prepare for the death of a spouse? I'm not sure we can do much beyond honestly realizing that someday it may happen. A good strategy is for couples to talk together about death and what life could look like as a single. Will it necessitate a move? If so, talk about where or what type of facility. What type of financial adjustments will be needed? It's wise to discuss such issues as funeral or memorial service arrangements, and choosing between burial or cremation. Purchasing burial plots and funeral services in advance can make the time of a spouse's death easier. The more of these things that are done in advance, the easier things are at the time.

Still, it's never easy to rebound after the death of your spouse. Life will never return to normal. Don't try to handle it on your own. Keep in touch with your church leaders, family, and friends. Share your feelings, request their prayers, and ask if they can refer you to a grief support group within the church or community that will help you adapt.

Other Challenges

You may experience many other challenges through your later years. Such things don't have a one-size-fits-all solution. Your best strategy is to continue to trust and depend on the Lord to an extent that will allow the most difficult challenges of life to draw you closer to him, and not push you away.

You're wise to develop a biblically based understanding of God well before such demanding challenges come. The reality is that once you're in such a challenging situation, it may be very difficult to learn to view God rightly.

One way to prepare for these difficulties is to read some good books now, such as *How Long, O Lord?* by D. A. Carson, *Walking with God through Pain and Suffering* by Timothy Keller, and *When God Weeps* by Joni Eareckson Tada and Steve Estes.

Adjust or Be Resilient

These hurdles will eventually either resolve themselves—allowing us, with God's help, to bounce back and be resilient—or they'll lead to permanent changes to which we must adjust. There are several keys to our being able to adjust or be resilient.

First, we must trust that God will use the difficulties we face to accomplish his good plans for us. Listen to Paul's hard experience:

> We do not want you to be unaware, brothers, of the affliction we experienced in Asia. For we were so utterly burdened beyond our strength that we despaired of life itself. Indeed, we felt that we had received the sentence of death. But that was to make us rely not on ourselves but on God who raises the dead. He delivered us from such a deadly peril, and he will deliver us. On him we have set our hope that he will deliver us again. You also must help us by prayer, so that many will give thanks on our behalf for the blessing granted us through the prayers of many. (2 Cor. 1:8–11)

Paul was grateful that God could be glorified through his excruciating trials, whether it was by his own reliance on God or in the thankfulness of those who were praying for him.

To trust God, we must believe that he's in control. What we're experiencing is not a tragic mistake but part of the loving plan that God will be sure to carry out, as he has promised. Take comfort in these two passages: "For I know the plans I have for you, declares the LORD, plans for welfare and not for evil, to give you a future and a hope" (Jer. 29:11) and "we know that for those who love God all things work together for good, for those who are called according to his purpose" (Rom. 8:28).

We can therefore respond in full assurance and faith:

O Lord, God of our fathers, are you not God in heaven? You rule over all the kingdoms of the nations. In your hand are power and might, so that none is able to withstand you. (2 Chron. 20:6)

I know that you can do all things, and that no purpose of yours can be thwarted. (Job 42:2)

Even as we trust God, we must also learn to lament. Old Testament scholar Tremper Longman defines lament as "a cry uttered when life falls apart."[3] When our lives are at that place, we must not respond with a fake smile and say that everything's going fine. Instead, we must be transparently honest with God and with others. We must cry to God in our distress, tell him that we're hurting, and plead for his help.

Lamenting is a practice we may be prone to overlook. We may prefer thinking of ourselves as somehow too spiritual to be overcome with sorrow, and we want others to see us that way as well. But how often in the Psalms do we see the writer crying out to God in his pain?

When David wrote Psalm 57, he was hiding in a cave from King Saul. With honesty, David laid his desperate situation before the Lord in lament:

My soul is in the midst of lions;
    I lie down amid fiery beasts. . . .
They set a net for my steps;

3 Tremper Longman III, *Jeremiah, Lamentations,* Understanding the Bible Commentary Series (Grand Rapids, MI: Baker, 2012), 330.

my soul was bowed down.

They dug a pit in my way. (Ps. 57:4, 6)

Or consider this striking lament:

Awake! Why are you sleeping, O Lord?

Rouse yourself! Do not reject us forever!

Why do you hide your face?

Why do you forget our affliction and oppression?

For our soul is bowed down to the dust;

our belly clings to the ground.

Rise up; come to our help!

Redeem us for the sake of your steadfast love!

(Ps. 44:23–26)

Challenges will come up that will make us question God's love and care. It will seem that he's sleeping and has rejected us. Those are the times when we're to cry out to him. He may seem to be sleeping, but he'll hear us and respond in the way that's best for us.

Recognizing God's love and sovereignty and learning to lament are important ways to adjust to the challenges that come in retirement. Fortunately, some challenges we face will resolve or become sufficiently stable to allow us to be resilient and get back to a normal life. Let me share three stories of resilience.

Those who watched the 2016 Rio Olympics will never forget the 10,000-meter run for the gold. Mo Farah, the British runner, fell midway through the race. He recovered, got up, joined the pack of other runners, and won the gold. Talk about resilience!

Ernest Gordon writes about God's work to transform a prisoner of war camp during World War II. You may be familiar with part of this story, as the setting was made famous by the 1957 movie

The Bridge on the River Kwai. The POW camp had been run in-humanely, with many of the prisoners dying from lack of food or care. Hate and atrocities were rampant. Then, miraculously, the Spirit of God moved in the camp, and the love of Christ began to change the atmosphere. Love often replaced hate, and self-sacrifice replaced selfishness. Hope was restored. The prisoners taught each other courses, started an orchestra, and staged plays. One play was a pantomime involving a skilled actor:

> Dressed as a scarecrow, he tumbled about in time to the music, as though buffeted by the wind. His gymnastic dexter-ity was earning him unusually loud and prolonged applause. A man in front of me leaned towards his neighbor and said in a low voice, "Just like life, ain't it?"
>
> The performer was much more than an acrobat—he was an artist. Throughout the dance of the scarecrow he was giving such an artistic interpretation of man's condition that it brought a strong response from the audience. . . .
>
> I listened again to the conversation in front of me. . . .
>
> "Yeah, the way he keeps getting knocked down, and then bobbing back like that, as though he's coming up for more."
>
> "Aye, he does that. He says to you that life *is* a knock-about, but you've got to keep going. It's the keeping going that makes him human, isn't it? Whenever he stops a bit, or lies down—he's just a scarecrow. Ain't that right?"[4]

My third example is a woman in her nineties I was sitting next to at a concert. I inquired about her life, and she told me

---

4 Ernest Gordon, *To End All Wars* (Grand Rapids, MI: Zondervan, 2002), 155. Originally published in Great Britain in 1963 as *Through the Valley of the Kwai,* then in 1965 as *Miracle on the River Kwai.*

she was married and had five children before her husband died when she was thirty. She raised their children singlehandedly, and when they were all through college, she remarried. With her new husband they refurbished a home near a college campus and housed international music students. Her second husband then died, and she continued to run her home as a boarding house. She encouraged and supported the students and attended their concerts.

Hearing all this, I said, "Wow, that's an amazing life!"

She responded, "No, I had five amazing lives."

What she had was resilience. She may have been knocked down, but she was able to get up and continue to live well. It's that type of resilience in retirement that can glorify God. The problem is that it's not our default. Too many of us are permanently set back by one defeat, and we stay defeated. We don't get up and get back in the race.

Adjusting and being resilient to the problems that come are essential throughout our later days. The question is, how? Where do we find the strength and desire to keep going? We often don't have that strength in ourselves, but we can look to God for it. Whether we need to adjust and live with the problem, or be resilient and bounce back, he has given us numerous resources to get us through. For instance, we have our friends—the brothers and sisters who become our support group. They're the ones who live out these instructions:

Rejoice with those who rejoice, weep with those who weep. (Rom.12:15)

Bear one another's burdens, and so fulfill the law of Christ. (Gal. 6:2)

We must be willing to share our needs with these friends, giving them the opportunity to serve Christ as they serve us.

We also have the presence of the Holy Spirit within us. He is our strength, our fortress, and our deliverer. We can trust him:

> For I, the LORD your God,
>   hold your right hand;
> it is I who say to you, "Fear not,
>   I am the one who helps you." (Isa. 41:13)

> Behold, I am with you always, to the end of the age. (Matt. 28:20)

> He who dwells in the shelter of the Most High
>   will abide in the shadow of the Almighty.
> I will say to the LORD, "My refuge and my fortress,
>   my God, in whom I trust." (Ps. 91:1–2)

Resilience comes also from knowing that at the end of our lives, we'll be with Jesus himself. God's grace trains us—as the apostle Paul reminds us—to be "waiting for our blessed hope, the appearing of the glory of our great God and Savior Jesus Christ" (Titus 2:13).

> So we are always of good courage. We know that while we are at home in the body we are away from the Lord, for we walk by faith, not by sight. Yes, we are of good courage, and we would rather be away from the body and at home with the Lord. (2 Cor. 5:6–8)

One of the rules we were all given when learning to drive was to keep our eyes on the road ahead, not on the pavement immediately in front of us. If we focus on what's immediately ahead, we begin to weave in our lane. If we focus on what's ahead in the distance, we can keep on track. So to overcome these late-in-life hurdles, focus on your future with Jesus.

Another source of resilience is a full-orbed prayer life. This includes the same elements of prayer that we discussed in strategy 5, but now with a specific new emphasis.

Adoration. We praise God that he's in full control of our final years, and is all-wise and loving.

Confession. We know we need to continue dealing with sin in our lives if we're going to keep going: "Let us also lay aside every weight and sin which clings so closely, and let us run with patience the race that is set before us" (Heb.12:1).

Thanksgiving. Even when we've experienced loss, we can still look back with gratitude for the many blessings we enjoy.

Supplication. We ask God for his grace to get through each day, allowing us to adjust and be resilient. We pray that he'll accomplish his purposes in allowing these losses.

Rebalance

Experiencing each of these hurdles will force us to find a new balance point for our priorities. As your strength and cognition diminish, or as you live now without your spouse, you may not be able to do the activities that God called you to previously. Whether you're adjusting to your new life or bouncing back from a difficult situation, things will be different. Glorifying God at this stage of your retirement may mean spending more time with Jesus, reading or hearing the Scriptures read, praying, and savoring our Lord's presence.

Those who've invested much time and energy serving their family may now allow the family to serve them. Their primary service may be to encourage and pray for those they love. In general, prayer may be a much more significant part of their lives.

Bill Bright was the founder of the college ministry now named Cru (formerly Campus Crusade for Christ). One of his friends told me that Bright spent his last two years confined to bed with a progressive disease of the lungs. He testified that because he was able to spend so much time in prayer, those were some of the richest years of his spiritual life.

I remember an amazing patient who had experienced years of crippling arthritis and was now confined to bed. She told me that she spent her sleepless nights praying. I asked who she was praying for, and she replied that it was for her family, for her nurses—and for me. What a blessing and encouragement that was for me!

Yes, retirement may have its surprises and challenges that make it a more difficult season to glorify God, but that's never going to be the end of the story. The end of retirement for those who have retired well will be to stand in the presence of Jesus and experience his glory in a way they could never do on this earth.

Let us long for—and live for— that day. That's the final strategy for a joyful, fulfilling retirement that brings glory to God.

Questions to Ponder

1. If you have retired, what stage of retirement are you in?

2. What challenges do you foresee ahead that will require your adjustment or resilience?

3. What resources should you begin to develop that will help you respond well?

4. Can you trust a God who puts you through difficult times? Why?

5. In light of what we've discussed for this strategy of being flexible, adaptable, and resilient, what changes are you committed to make in your life?

PRAYER

Gracious heavenly Father, I thank you for the option of retirement. I want to approach it cautiously, for it's a valuable gift you're giving me. Above all else, I want my years in retirement to give you glory. Help me see how everything I do can lead to this. When I face changes along the way, allow me to keep on track, savor your presence, and adjust and be resilient.

I pray this for the sake of my Lord and Savior, Jesus Christ. In his name. Amen.

Recommended Reading

Relevant Christian Books

Don't Waste Your Life by John Piper (Crossway, updated edition, 2009)

Finishing Our Course with Joy: Guidance from God for Engaging with Our Aging by J. I. Packer (Crossway, 2014)

God Isn't Finished with Me Yet: Discovering the Spiritual Graces of Later Life by Barbara Lee (Loyola Press, 2018)

How to Finish the Christian Life: Following Jesus in the Second Half by Donald W. Sweeting and George Sweeting (Moody, 2012)

Rethinking Retirement: Finishing Life for the Glory of Christ by John Piper (Crossway, 2009)

An Uncommon Guide to Retirement: Finding God's Purpose for the Next Season of Life by Jeff Haanen (Moody, 2019)

Christian Financial Advice for Retirement

Biblical Retirement: Preparing for a Christian's Retirement by Richard L. Baker (2015, CreateSpace)

The Burkett & Blue Definitive Guide to Securing Wealth to Last: Money Essentials for the Second Half of Life by Larry Burkett and Ron Blue (B&H, 2003)

Reimagine Retirement: Planning and Living for the Glory of God by C. J. Cagle (B&H, 2019)

Other Resources

The Joy of Retirement: Finding Happiness, Freedom, and the Life You've Always Wanted by David C. Borchard with Patricia A. Donohoe (Amacom, 2008)

Purposeful Retirement: How to Bring Happiness and Meaning to Your Retirement by Hyrum W. Smith (Mango, 2017)

The Retirement Challenge: A Non-financial Guide from Top Retirement Experts by various members of the Retirement Coaches Association (Robert Laura, 2018)

Retirement and Its Discontents: Why We Won't Stop Working Even If We Can by Michelle Pannor Silver (Columbia University Press, 2018)

Retirement Your Way: The No Stress Roadmap for Designing Your Next Chapter and Loving Your Future by Gail M. McDonald and Marilyn L. Bushey (Choices Next, 2019)

What Will I Do All Day? Wisdom to Get You Over Retirement and On with Living! Patrice Jenkins (Engelsen, 2011)

General Index

Scripture Index

Also Available from John Dunlop, MD

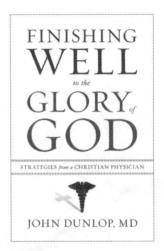

For more information, visit **crossway.org**.